In *7 Traits of Effective Parenting* Daniel Huerta hits that rare sweet spot of "deep and wide." Like a skilled conductor, he orchestrates the big sound of seven key movements but then spotlights numerous small instruments of practical, easily understood applications that make creating our own family symphony seem possible. You'll be inspired and equipped as you listen to and then apply this fine work.

GARY THOMAS
Author of *Sacred Marriage: What If God Designed Marriage to Make Us Holy More Than to Make Us Happy?* and *Sacred Parenting: How Raising Children Shapes Our Souls*

Moms and Dads—this book is worth reading. The content won't overwhelm you. Danny's stories will encourage you, and his thought-provoking analogies, relevant and realistic exercises, and complete ideas will inspire you to grow. I also love his use of Scripture! Danny's counseling background and love for God qualify him to write this important and empowering roadmap to parenting success. No matter the ages of your children or if you've experienced some major challenges or not, you'll discover you can develop the 7 traits. You'll want to!

DR. KATHY KOCH
Founder/President of Celebrate Kids, Inc., cofounder of Ignite the Family, and author of *8 Great Smarts: Discover and Nurture Your Child's Intelligences* and *Screens and Teens: Connecting with Our Kids in a Wireless World.*

There are a lot of books out there on the topic of parenting. I should know, I've written a few myself! This one, complete with Scripture, is a good resource for Christian parents.

DR. KEVIN LEMAN
New York Times bestselling author of *Have a New Kid by Friday*

Every parent I know is looking for help in raising children. Danny Huerta coaches us as moms and dads with the profound insights he's gained from his years as a family therapist and the timeless wisdom of God's Word. I love how practical and accessible this book is!

BOB LEPINE
Cohost, FamilyLife Today

With personal anecdotes and applicable Scripture, Daniel Huerta lays out useful and realistic guidelines to better parenting. Not just another book on parenting, it looks deeper while providing practical ways to apply the wisdom that is, at times, right in front of our eyes. Great job, Daniel!

MARK HANCOCK
CEO, Trail Life USA

7 Traits of Effective Parenting is like family counseling, with all of the wisdom and none of the commute. I've already begun incorporating some of the exercises and illustrations with my own family, and I'm a better parent for it. Whether you're a new parent or a seasoned veteran, you're sure to encounter some "aha" moments as you read this valuable resource.

JESSIE MINASSIAN
Author

As a parent, I am always looking for great tools to empower my parenting and to gain wisdom. If you can relate to me in this way, I would recommend Daniel Huerta's fabulous book *7 Traits of Effective Parenting*. With practical stories, relevant Scriptures, and truths he's learned from his very effective practice, Daniel provides encouragement and help for all parents in all stages of the journey!

REBECCA ST. JAMES
Christian singer-songwriter and author

FOCUS ON THE FAMILY

PRESENTS

SEVEN TRAITS OF EFFECTIVE PARENTING

DANIEL P. HUERTA
MSW, LCSW, VP OF PARENTING

Tyndale House Publishers
Carol Stream, Illinois

FOCUS ON THE FAMILY® | FOCUS ON PARENTING™

Cover design by Mitch Bolton

Interior illustrations by Mitch Bolton and Michael Harrigan

I dedicate this book to my wife, Heather, who has loved me and come alongside me in this imperfect and exciting journey of marriage and raising our children. I love you and thank you for your hard work and dedication to a spiritual foundation in our home.

To my two kids, Alex and Lexi, who are truly incredible gifts from God. There are several stories in this book displaying God's transformation of us through you and you through us. What a joy it is for us to be your parents. I'm thankful for the many things we have learned and enjoyed along the way, and I'm looking forward to more.

To my parents, Carol and Ricardo, who worked hard at providing a spiritual foundation for our family growing up and faithfully prayed for each of us every day. Thank you for your love, sacrifices, guidance, and great memories.

To my mother- and father-in-law, Rita and Don. You have been patient, loving, and generous toward me. I love seeing how you love your daughters. Thank you for raising a daughter whom I love and for providing a spiritual foundation for her from the time she was a little girl.

CONTENTS

PREFACE

I'VE KNOWN DANNY HUERTA for many years now as a member of our team at Focus on the Family. As our Vice President of Parenting and Youth, he has lent his voice to our radio program numerous times and spearheaded important programs, including *Alive to Thrive*, a suicide-prevention resource for parents and youth leaders, and *Launch into the Teen Years*, a comprehensive primer for that critical stage, including the topic of sexuality, for parents and preteens. He has also been interviewed by Fox News, *Christianity Today*, and numerous other outlets, and has written for the *Washington Post*.

If you've never had the chance to "hear" from Danny through Focus on the Family or one of those other venues, I'm pleased that you'll now have the opportunity to do so within the pages of this, his very first book. There is great wisdom and practical application to be found here, informed by Danny's years of experience as a school social worker and licensed clinical social worker counseling families, and his ongoing pursuit of a doctorate in psychology at California Southern University.

Those are important credentials, but the title Danny wears most proudly is "dad." He and his wife, Heather, are the parents of two wonderful children, Alex and Lexi. More than his extensive clinical and professional experience, what you'll find in this book are the honest and heartfelt words of someone who is in the throes of raising kids, just like you are. As you read, you'll likely find yourself nodding in recognition as Danny describes the joys and challenges he and Heather have encountered in their own parenting journey.

Although it is built upon a solid foundation of research and experience, *7 Traits of Effective Parenting* is not an academic, clinical textbook written by someone who is disconnected from the subject matter. It's more like a conversation— sometimes funny and always practical—with a parent and family therapist who is in the trenches *with* you, doing his best to raise children "in the discipline and instruction of the Lord" (Ephesians 6:4) and to counsel families through God's unending and trustworthy wisdom.

I can't think of a better recommendation than that, and I believe the combination of those two elements—clinical expertise and real-world practicality—makes *7 Traits of Effective Parenting* an indispensable resource for any parent. I hope you'll agree.

Jim Daly
President, Focus on the Family

FOREWORD

THERE'S SOMETHING AMAZING popping up on college campuses across the country. At UC Berkeley, students are lining up to take an "adulting" class. The same thing is happening at the "Adulting School" in Portland, Maine. Across the country, young men and women are looking for help filling in something that's missing from their lives.

What's missing are core skills related to growing up and doing relationships well—the kind of bonding and wise-living actions you'd think everyone would have seen in their homes growing up. But in today's world, you'd be wrong. That's because there's a crucial thing missing in many homes today: *modeling*—that gift of watching someone, up close and personal, do life well.

Like so many, I was desperate for a model. My emotional balance sheet was heavily weighted toward brokenness rather than health. Without a father in the home and with my mother sick or gone a great deal of the time, I was left with television and other lost friends as my role models. This combination of circumstances left me, as a young man, feeling that there was no way I could ever be successful at marriage. Much less could I imagine being a father who didn't totally ruin his kids. It was like facing the future with at least one relational arm tied behind my back.

But then I walked into a home like Danny Huerta's.

Not literally *Danny's* home. You see, as I read this helpful, practical, encouraging book, I was reminded over and over again of an incredible gift God gave me, which was the opportunity to walk into the home of a family that modeled health and connection.

For me, that family was the Barrams. Their home was genuinely filled with light and love. It was a home with parents who lived with wisdom and related to their family members with honor and encouragement. Not perfectly. But there was humor, connection, and correction without shame or anger. I would walk away from each visit to the Barrams' home saying to myself, "So that's how you do that!" And at an even deeper level, "And that's how I'm going to do it one day with my family!" What a gift that was!

With this book, let me invite you to walk into the Huerta home. It's a visit (and book) based around seven words. He calls them "traits." Each is foundational for healthy relating. And each trait is based on Scripture, sound science, and great counseling insights from a master counselor. But it's not just the solid information I found so helpful. It's all the "Here's how the Huerta family lives this out" sidebars and examples that put a "can't miss" face on health and love.

If you're like me, the struggle isn't with the question "Are these traits true?" I'd love to have each trait reflected in my home and life. But rather, the difficulty is in "How do you live out these traits in real life?" Figuring this out is what's important if they're to truly transfer to my home—and to yours.

So enjoy your visit to the Huerta family. Like the Barrams, they're not perfect. But their story, and these seven traits, are perfectly timed for families like mine, and I think for your family as well.

John Trent, PhD
President, StrongFamilies.com

FROM KNOWLEDGE TO WISDOM

*You shall love the LORD your God with all your heart
and with all your soul and with all your might. And
these words that I command you today shall be on your
heart. You shall teach them diligently to your children,
and shall talk of them when you sit in your house, and
when you walk by the way, and when you lie down,
and when you rise.*

–DEUTERONOMY 6:5-7

THE JOB OF PARENTING IS especially difficult today because the adversity we face is complex. There seem to be more disasters, tragedies, temptations, distractions, and stress than ever before. And we have access to more information about these events than ever before in history. The more concerning thing is the way society is pushing God out of the center. Our culture today is trying to redefine just about everything, including love and truth. Our culture turns to knowledge, popularity, and academic degrees to find answers.

But God tells us that knowledge must be in step with

wisdom, otherwise it is useless. You can live by another man's knowledge, but not his wisdom. Wisdom is our own, and it ultimately comes from a close relationship with God. He is the Living Water and He is necessary for our survival. That's why He instructs us to desire His wisdom more than anything.

Parenting is a deeply transformative process. I believe God created family to provide us with opportunities for amazing growth and transformation. When we are transformed by our growth as parents, we become more deeply rooted in God's wisdom and will be more equipped to guide our kids toward God's original plan of us being contributors within His Kingdom.

From the beginning, God wanted us to be contributors within His Kingdom story and not consumers. The moment Adam and Eve chose to consume the fruit out of a lack of trust, we became consumers in a garden needing contributors. As we contribute to our kids through our parenting, we guide our kids toward becoming contributors to others and to the overall functioning of the family and society, thus fulfilling their role in God's Kingdom story.

Unfortunately, though, many parents strive too hard for perfection, somehow thinking that perfect parenting is a destination—that we "win" if we are perfect or have well-behaved kids. However, the Bible is full of less-than-stellar examples of parenting. Consider Adam and Eve. The very first parents display for us an imperfect and messy home. The truth is that all parenting is imperfect and messy.

In reality, we "win" as parents if our children see God's transformative power, love, and influence in our lives. Effective parenting means learning to navigate and respond to the many imperfections that are a reality to all homes. Imperfections help us truly learn how to love and be loved. Imperfections help us learn the depth of our need for God.

We cannot control what our kids choose to do and what they will grow up to be, but we can certainly influence them through the minute-by-minute, hour-by-hour, and day-to-day interactions we have with them for eighteen-plus years, reminding them to be contributors rather than consumers. We cannot create perfect children, but we can certainly guide them along the way by how we live our own lives. We can leave imprints on their lives by how we communicate, interact, teach, guide, correct, and love.

This book is a practical journey through seven powerful traits that will help you be the most effective parent you can be. My goal is to provide a simple framework for you to grow in your parenting journey. As we grow in the seven traits of effective parenting, we can impart these same traits to our kids.

The seven traits of effective parenting are well researched and are based on the foundations provided through Scripture, my training and practice as a counselor serving families for more than two decades, and the great research surrounding the authoritative style of parenting.

INFO

Find out how you score in each of the seven traits of effective parenting by taking the self-assessment at FocusOnTheFamily.com /7traits.

The seven traits are:

- Adaptability
- Respect
- Intentionality
- Steadfast love
- Boundaries
- Grace and forgiveness
- Gratitude

My prayer is that this book is encouraging, practical, and helpful in your parenting adventure.

CHAPTER 1

CONTRIBUTORS, ENCOURAGERS, AND INFLUENCERS

You yourselves are our letter of recommendation, written on our hearts, to be known and read by all. And you show that you are a letter from Christ delivered by us, written not with ink but with the Spirit of the living God, not on tablets of stone but on tablets of human hearts.

–2 CORINTHIANS 3:2-3

HAVE YOU EVER SAT THROUGH the credits at the end of a film? While we may connect a particular movie with a big Hollywood star or a famous director, in reality hundreds, if not thousands, of people are involved in making a movie. The rolling credits of some films take ten minutes or more to scroll through because everyone involved in making the movie is mentioned in the credits, from the actors, directors, and producers to the people who created the special effects, created the costumes, and catered the lunches. It is awe-inspiring to think about the hundreds of people and thousands of hours of work that are required to produce a movie.

In a similar way, none of us is completely self-made. All of us have, in a sense, rolling credits made up of all the people who have made a difference in our lives. Perhaps a coach contributed countless hours teaching you to shoot free throws. You may remember the encouragement of a piano teacher as you struggled to learn a difficult piece. Maybe an elder in your church influenced you with his faithful service to God over the years. Hundreds of people have played a role in the shaping of you. All of them are part of your rolling credits.

OUR ROLLING CREDITS BEGIN WITH GOD

God is the Master Architect of our lives. From conception to eternity, God has a plan for each of us. The Bible says that He formed us in our mothers' wombs. He knows the number of hairs on our heads and how many days have been allotted to us. He determined both the times and the places where we each live. He provides salvation for us and plans good works for us to do. He provides a great inheritance for us as coheirs of His Kingdom. He has gone ahead of us to prepare a place in eternity for us.

God provides opportunities for us to have contributors, influencers, and encouragers in this world—just as He did for the difference makers in the Bible.

- He provided David with an influencer named Nathan, who helped David open his eyes, spiritually speaking, to what he had done as he pursued Bathsheba.

- Josiah was positively influenced as a young child. That influence helped him remain committed to God when he became the king of Israel as a boy.

- Shadrach, Meshach, and Abednego almost certainly had incredible contributors, encouragers, and influencers in their young lives, judging by how they confidently lived out their faith and remained steadfast in their love of God.

- Mordecai contributed to Esther's life and encouraged and influenced her as she obediently followed the plan God had set before her.

OUR ROLLING CREDITS AID OUR GROWTH

Picture a city that is growing. It is always under construction and has countless people who help it grow. In the same way, countless people help us to grow. Contributors pour resources into our lives that subsidize our development. Encouragers give us boosts of strength and courage that keep us moving forward despite disappointments and setbacks. Influencers cast a vision of what a well-lived life looks like and show us how to live that life in practical ways.

These people who make up our rolling credits help us follow the advice from 2 Timothy 3:14: "But as for you, continue in what you have learned and have firmly believed, knowing from whom you learned it."

OUR ROLLING CREDITS HELP US LIVE A LEGACY

In Hebrews 12:1 the author urges, "Therefore, since we are surrounded by so great a cloud of witnesses, let us also lay aside every weight, and sin which clings so closely, and let us run with endurance the race that is set before us."

The rolling credits of our lives stretch backward in time as we look to those who have lived faithful lives for God in the past. These are the ones who ran the race with endurance and passed the baton to us. But rolling credits also stretch forward in time as we look toward those we can contribute to, encourage, and influence. These are the ones to whom we must pass the baton as we run our own races of faithful endurance.

As a contributor, encourager, and influencer using the seven traits of effective parenting, you can help your child run the race that is set before him or her. And thus, the legacy continues onward until the Lord returns. A great way to prepare yourself for that task is to take a look at those you have listened to along the way.

CONTRIBUTORS

Contributors are people who have poured their time, energy, talents, money, and attention into you. These people can include your spouse, coaches, grandparents, aunts, uncles, cousins, siblings, teachers, parents, friends, mentors, and life coaches. The Christian life is full of contributors.

- King Darius contributed to Daniel's life and gave him the highest position in the kingdom.

- Jesus contributed to the lives of His disciples to equip them for God's work.

- People all around the world contribute to missionaries as they carry out God's work and calling.

I recall the phone conversation I had as a sophomore with the tennis coach at my high school. He said I should try out for the tennis team. I remember laughing at his suggestion because I was awful at tennis. I shared with him that I had just gotten back from a trip to visit my relatives in Mexico and had played tennis with my cousin, Carlos. I had a difficult time keeping the ball in the court. At this particular club, a ball boy was assigned to retrieving the tennis balls for the players. Well, this ball boy got an incredible workout that day—not to mention a great tip. I had to bounce the ball to serve and I hit most balls off the rim of the racket. It really wasn't pretty.

But the coaches at my school invested a lot of their time and energy in teaching me how to improve my tennis skills. They saw something in me that I didn't see. I ended up as the third singles player on the varsity team my senior year. I was not an amazing player, but I came to be a decent player with a killer serve, and I received a tennis scholarship. I continue to play tennis with friends whenever I can. And I'm working to pass on my love for tennis to my own kids. The

Date Nights

One way to contribute to your family is to plan special evenings together. Date night is a time for connection, conversation, and speaking truth into your child. Dates with your child may involve a walk or a bike ride together. You might draw together or go to a sporting event. Recently our family went to a restaurant. My daughter and I sat at one table, and my son and wife sat at another table. This allowed us to give special attention to each of our children.

Keep in mind that dates can be creative, simple, and inexpensive, but they can also be elaborate and expensive. Date nights are all about investing in relationships. The possibilities are nearly endless. You could

contribution of two men gave me something besides money for college: I've been privileged to pay it forward and teach the kids I work with to never say never.

Sometimes other people can see something in us that we can't see. Throughout my childhood, my mom and dad contributed their money, time, and energy toward my development. I didn't always see or acknowledge their contributions. But now I can see it. And now I can pass on that gift as I contribute my money, time, and energy to others.

If you look carefully, you will see that many people have contributed to your life. It's great to look back with gratitude. Now is your opportunity to look forward and contribute to the lives of your own children.

For every positive type of role model, there is a counter or negative role model. The opposite of being a contributor to someone's life is being a consumer in someone's life.

Consumers are people who tend to use you for their own gain. They approach you with a personal shopping list in mind as they interact with you. Everyone has experienced having consumers in their lives. If we're honest, most of us have acted like consumers at one point or another in other people's rolling credits.

Being a consumer comes naturally in our instant-gratification, live-for-yourself, pursue-personal-success-and-happiness culture. We want to be loved, noticed, and admired without wanting to contribute to other people.

In a recent survey, 49 percent of teens said they post about their own accomplishments on social media.[1] Teens are thirsty to be known and recognized. In addition, in a different survey, 45 percent of teens said they are stressed all the time.[2] Teens need encouragement and help coping with demands and expectations they feel incapable of living up to or fulfilling.[3]

You can help counter these influences by sincerely contributing to the lives of the kids you know. Help

take some time to talk to your kids about people who have contributed to your life, encouraged you, or influenced you along the way. You can also ask them who they have seen as contributors, encouragers, and influencers in their lives so far.

kids find genuine encouragement rather than needing to seek it out. Through your own example, teach them to be noticers and celebrators of other people's accomplishments, skills, and talents. Looking beyond "self" helps to reduce stress. Help children be noticers of:

- people who are thirsty for God's love and hope
- people who are orphaned or widowed
- people who need encouragement or a listening ear

Your positive example in this area can help kids discern where to invest their own time, attention, skills, and energy. This helps to build a contributor mindset in your children.

ENCOURAGERS

Encouragers are people who offer words of support and inspiration that build others up.

During my senior year of high school, I was walking in the hall when the principal stopped me and said, "You are going to be a great leader someday." I still remember that very brief interaction to this day. His words encouraged me then, and they still encourage me today.

My mom and dad have encouraged me along the way, for which I am very thankful. In fact, my dad continues to write me a letter of encouragement once or twice a year. His encouraging words have been like a cup of cold water after a hot summer run. My mom carefully selects cards for my birthday or Father's Day to provide me with encouraging words on those occasions.

Encouraging words are always welcome! Why don't we offer them more often? My wife has sometimes said to me that she wants more encouraging words from me. It is so easy to forget to consistently speak encouraging words to my wife and my children. All I can say is that it is good that we get a new day every twenty-four hours so I can try again. It is like God built a reset button into each day. His mercies are new every morning! Go ahead and press your own reset button today.

The opposite of being an encourager is being a discourager. While encouraging words can be seen as building blocks in a person's life, discouraging words can be the destroyers. I vividly recall an incident that happened when my son and daughter were much younger. My son, Alex, was building with Legos when suddenly my daughter, Lexi, came by and, in an instant,

ACTIVITY

Journal Notes

My teenage son and daughter enjoy getting notes. We each have a journal at our spot on the kitchen table. Anyone can write in anyone else's journal. I frequently will write a note or a quotation or draw something for my kids and my wife (though not every day). The notes don't have to be long. My son, daughter, and wife all love words of encouragement that are genuine and authentic. We all treasure these journals as we record encouraging words to one another throughout the year.

Filled Cup

Gather a disposable cup, superhero stickers, and your child's favorite sweet beverage.

Explain to your child that the cup represents him or her. Read Psalm 18:29, Colossians 1:29, and Ephesians 3:20-21 from an easy-to-understand Bible translation. Tell your child that God says we can do amazing things with His strength. Discuss God's amazing strength. Encourage your child to decorate the cup with superhero stickers to represent God's strength in his or her life.

Read Ephesians 2:10. Talk about the good works (contributions) that God wants your child to do—these good works were planned by God specifically for your child. Discuss how this relates to being half destroyed what had taken Alex a long time to build.

Encouragers and discouragers in our lives tend to run along similar lines. It takes us a long time to trust the encouraging words, while discouraging words tend to have an immediate and lasting negative impact on us. We tend to be more attentive to negative criticism.

Keep in mind, however, that discouragement is different from constructive criticism. Discouragement is meant to tear down, to demean, and to belittle. Constructive criticism is helpful for growth and building—it's a necessary, but difficult, part of parenting. When we offer constructive criticism to our children, we must keep in mind the apostle Paul's admonition to speak the truth in love (Ephesians 4:15).

Consider your own words. Do you use your words to tear down or to build up? How can you more effectively and consistently encourage those in your family? Contributors build and consumers tear down.

Contributors want the well-being of the other while consumers desire their own well-being.

INFLUENCERS

In the spring of 1983, my parents decided to move our family to the United States. I had lived in Mexico City, Mexico, my entire eight years of life.

My mom said, "You need to say goodbye to your friends. You won't see them again. We are moving to Colorado."

I didn't know what that meant. I had never heard of Colorado, but I did know that my mom had tried to teach me English. She had been a persistent influence in my life as she and my dad prepared me for the transition to the United States.

The summer of 1983 was a challenging but powerful time in my life. I spent the summer with my English-speaking grandparents, uncle, and aunts in Minnesota while my parents moved to Colorado

a contributor rather than a consumer. Also discuss the role God might want your child to assume in the world. Explain that God fills us with His strength and goodness and helps us to serve others.

Fill the cup with your child's favorite sweet beverage. Tell your child that as we read Scripture and have ongoing dialogue with God, our cups are filled with His love and strength. Explain to your child that once the cup of his or her life is filled with God's strength and goodness, your child will be able to effectively serve others with the sweetness of God's love. Discuss how your child can encourage and influence others with God's love. Encourage your child to enjoy the beverage.

Springs with my older brother and sister. I couldn't really understand what people were saying and learned to listen carefully that summer. I watched as my grandparents knelt beside their bed together and prayed for people individually and by name. I remember them kneeling for a long time each time they prayed. Similarly, my parents faithfully prayed together before bed. I could hear them praying as I fell asleep across the hall. The examples of my grandparents and parents had a profound influence on my life. Today, prayer is a centerpiece in my home.

That summer, my grandpa taught me about gardening and loving God. My grandma loved the kitchen and served the family faithfully. There was no dishwasher, so we each had a responsibility. My time in Minnesota helped me learn how to help in the kitchen and with everyday chores. My grandparents had a direct and lasting influence on my life.

You *will* have a lasting influence in your child's life. But what kind of impact will you leave? I strongly believe that parents who grow in the seven traits of effective parenting will have a profoundly positive influence in their children's lives. Parenting is about contributing, encouraging, and influencing and not about being perfect.

The opposite of being an influencer is being a distractor. Distractors are those who have a negative effect on others' lives.

The world is full of competing influences at unprecedented levels. Some research suggests that kids turn to screens to get away from a chaotic world.[4] Wisdom is essential as you sort through the influences to figure out what is truly worthwhile and what is simply a distraction. It is your privilege and responsibility to teach and model for your children what it means to navigate a world full of influencers and distractors. Though Solomon was wise, distractors lured him away from God's wisdom and call on his life (Nehemiah 13:26). He was swayed by a distracted consumer mindset rather than the focused, wise, contributor mindset God had called him to live out. The accumulation of little decisions we make ends up creating the overall direction of our lives.

Keep in mind that marital stress and children who act out can quickly distract us in our parenting. When there is marital stress, research suggests that dads tend to disengage and become avoidant, while mothers tend to become more controlling and strict.[5] It is also interesting that stress in the marriage makes parents less consistent in their parenting and support. The same research found that consistent involvement, boundaries, and support from parents resulted in

ACTIVITY

Rolling Credits Party

Invite your contributors, encouragers, and influencers to a party to celebrate their impact in your life. It would be great for your kids to meet these builders in your life. Talk about ways they affected your life. Kids need to see that it takes many people—with God as the cornerstone— to build a life.

Another option is to write notes of appreciation to the many people who have been a part of your rolling credits.

fewer problem behaviors in teenagers. This positive influence helps keep teenagers on track during this turbulent and confusing time of life.

• • •

I was recently at the funeral of a man who lived out his role as husband, father, and grandfather the best he could. I enjoyed listening to the testimonies that were shared about his life. The common thread in what was said was not that he was perfect but that he tried his best to love his family by being as consistent as possible and spending time with them. He had taken the time to be a contributor, encourager, and influencer in the lives of others. He was a part of the rolling credits in many people's lives. I'm sure he wasn't always loving, respectful, grateful, adaptable, forgiving, intentional, or great with boundaries, but he clearly tried his best.

As you read this book and learn about the seven traits of effective parenting, may you

be strengthened with power through his Spirit in your inner being, so that Christ may dwell in your hearts through faith—that you, being rooted and grounded in love, may have strength to comprehend with all the saints what is the breadth and length and height and depth, and to know the love of Christ that surpasses knowledge, that you may be filled with all the fullness of God. Now to him who is able to do far more abundantly than all that we ask or think, according to the power at work within us, to him be glory in the church and in Christ Jesus throughout all generations, forever and ever. Amen. (Ephesians 3:16-21)

CONTRIBUTORS, ENCOURAGERS, & INFLUENCERS

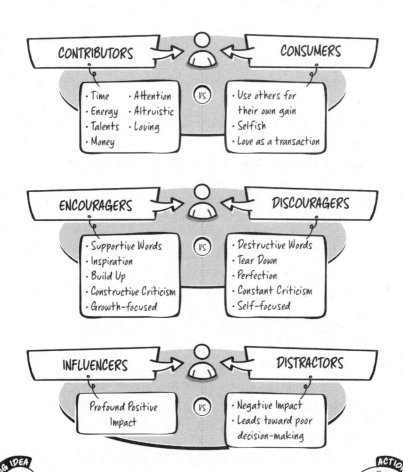

CONTRIBUTORS → ← **CONSUMERS**

VS

- Time
- Energy
- Talents
- Money
- Attention
- Altruistic
- Loving

- Use others for their own gain
- Selfish
- Love as a transaction

ENCOURAGERS → ← **DISCOURAGERS**

VS

- Supportive Words
- Inspiration
- Build Up
- Constructive Criticism
- Growth-focused

- Destructive Words
- Tear Down
- Perfection
- Constant Criticism
- Self-focused

INFLUENCERS → ← **DISTRACTORS**

VS

- Profound Positive Impact

- Negative Impact
- Leads toward poor decision-making

BIG IDEA

As a parent, you get to be a **CONTRIBUTOR, ENCOURAGER,** and **INFLUENCER** in the lives of your children as you lead them toward becoming contributors within God's Kingdom story.

ACTIONS

Model taking the time to be thankful for the contributors, encouragers, and influencers in your own life. Also model an awareness of the consumers, discouragers, and distractors in your own life.

CHAPTER 2

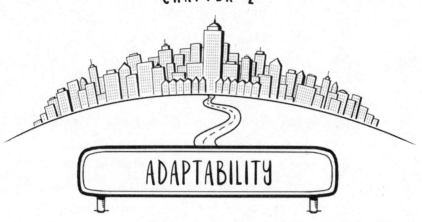

ADAPTABILITY

Change is the only constant in life.
One's ability to adapt to those changes will
determine your success in life.
–BENJAMIN FRANKLIN

Life isn't about waiting for the storm to pass.
It's about learning how to dance in the rain.
–VIVIAN GREENE

IN SCIENCE FICTION, adaptability is often presented in a caution-
ary manner. An artificial intelligence becomes a threat to
humanity when it learns to "read" a complex set of circumstances and adjust its actions accordingly. The more adaptable
the AI becomes, the more human—and then superhuman—it
becomes. In sci-fi, that's when the excitement and the danger
of the plot really kick in.

In real life, though, adaptability is one of the most valuable qualities a person can possess. Adaptability is the capac-
ity to adjust to all kinds of circumstances and to manage

the mind's response to whatever a person is facing at the moment.

Adaptability is also one of the most elusive qualities. In order to be adaptable, we must be able to assess and accept others as they are. Not as we assume they are or as we would like them to be, but as they really are. For most people, that's not easy because we tend to see others through the lens of our own experiences. While our bodies are incredibly designed to adapt, our minds sometimes prevent us from adapting well to new situations and unexpected circumstances. Deep emotions, personality differences, time constraints, and preconceived expectations are just a few of the factors that make it difficult to be adaptable.

To get an idea of how difficult adaptability can be, consider the issue of personality differences. There are a variety of tests that determine a person's personality type. Yet even the most sophisticated of them reveal only a quick glimpse into the complexity of an individual's own personality and how his or her personality interrelates with others.

Some personality types—for example, the flexible, the adventurous, the social, the spontaneous, and those less attentive to detail—are better equipped to be naturally adaptable. People at the other end of the spectrum—the inflexible, the safety-conscious, the opinionated, the traditional, and those more attentive to detail—find it more difficult to be adaptable. When you combine family members with variations of these personality traits, you get encounters that are ripe for stress.

I vividly remember a phone call I answered while serving in the counseling department at Focus on the Family. The mother on the line was screaming and crying. She had locked herself in the bathroom. I could hear her children calling for her and knocking on the door. She said she was done and couldn't do it anymore. She wanted to beat her children and had locked herself in the bathroom to protect them. She was exhausted, lonely, and completely overwhelmed. To start, we talked about what had led to that moment. After she calmed down, she was able to regain perspective and adapt to the trying situation she faced by implementing a different set of strategies. She needed to introduce structure to the chaos. She needed a plan to deal with her own emotions and to more effectively influence her children's responses to her. I thank God for that divine appointment and for the opportunity to help her from hundreds of miles away through the telephone!

Over the years, I have spoken with parents in many situations that were difficult to adapt to—everything from a child taking his own life to sharing chores as new parents to schedules packed with endless activities to a child being diagnosed with autism, depression, or obsessive-compulsive disorder. The variety of situations that parents must adapt and respond to is endless. And the challenge is that being adaptable means knowing that many times when we have a plan, the plan inevitably changes.

Recently I was standing in church, with my eyes closed, singing along with a praise chorus, when I felt a tap on my shoulder. My son asked, "Dad, can we talk?" This was the second time in the past year that my teenage son had asked for us to do this together at church. What an honor and unexpected surprise! My plan was to sing and spend some time with God. I wasn't fully prepared for my son's request, but I was certainly available. This was my son's journey intersecting with my availability. There is nothing that can fully prepare us for all the ins and outs of our kids' needs. We simply can't predict what they'll need and when they'll need it. They will need moments of warmth, sensitivity, and playfulness as well as moments of boundaries, demands, guidance, and focus. This can't be planned for, so we must adapt by being prepared and available to respond to these unexpected moments in our kids' lives.

UNDER CONSTRUCTION

In my counseling practice, the analogy that I use for adaptability involves, of all things, city planning and roadwork. If you've driven any distance lately, chances are good that you encountered some kind of roadwork. No matter where you go, something is always under construction. And to get where you want to go, you have to adapt to the roadblocks and detours that construction creates.

The same is true for families. Visualize a state map—this represents your family. Within the map, each family member is represented by a city. So in my family's state map, there are four cities, which represent me, my wife, my son, and my daughter. My family's state is characterized by my family's traits, and each city in my family's state is characterized by the unique traits of each family member. From each of the cities in your family's state, imagine drawing roads or major highways to connect the cities, depending on the strength of the connections between family members.

When a husband and wife first get together, they bring their past experiences, which include connections (roadways) to cities in other states and the unique characteristics that have been built into their own cities.

Think about when you first started dating your spouse. You visited each other's cities for the first time and loved what you saw. The more you spent time in each other's cities, the more you connected. With all of that traffic, however, came the need for roadwork. There were bound to be accidents and deterioration of the roads over time. It took time and intentionality as you adapted to one another's differences and decided to get married and build a permanent major highway between the two of you.

As two spouses build a major highway they establish stronger connections with each other over time. The husband and wife significantly and directly influence the development of one another's cities. They also can take characteristics of each other into their own cities. However, it is inevitable that there will need to be ongoing and constant repair, construction, and awareness from both as they adjust to each other's differences and work to maintain and expand a thriving highway connecting the two of them. Each of them will also need to have awareness of what it is like for others to visit their city. Is it ready for visitors? Do people feel welcomed, important, and loved as they enter the city? What other connections need to continue, be downsized, or be cut off? These are all important questions a couple needs to ask as they begin to establish an expanding and healthy state.

The couple's children begin as small cities with dirt roads initially connecting them to their parents and then to others around them. The more time, warmth, and attention are given to the children, the faster highways are built. The development of the children's cities is directly influenced through these relational highways. Kids learn the ins and outs of building and maintaining their own cities. Their cities, under constant construction, also take on unique characteristics.

God, in all of this, is the Master Architect, Designer, and Builder of both the cities and the highway systems. He has already mapped out the ultimate construction plan for each person. He loves to be a part of the foundational development of cities and highways. The more and the earlier kids learn to invite God's presence into the construction of their cities and roadways, the stronger and better developed they will be. God, through the death of His Son on the cross, initiated the ultimate highway-repair system. He introduced grace and forgiveness as essential ingredients for road repair between cities.

Keep in mind that some highways are bigger and better maintained than others. Some highways may have well-functioning bridges, while others have dilapidated or broken bridges. Through our parenting, kids learn that building and maintaining their cities is up to them. They also learn that maintenance, repair, and construction of highways to other cities is up to them. For example, a child can learn that sleep and proper nutrition help with overall city maintenance, and taking the time to reflect on his or her thoughts, feelings, and beliefs is like creating overall structure to the city.

The analogy raises a few questions:

- What happens when a city is cut off from other cities?
- What happens when there is very little traffic from others into a city?

- What happens if a person never builds or maintains his or her city?
- Is my city ready for a visit and connection with others?
- What will another person experience when they visit my city?
- What is the theme of my city?
- What do I want my city to resemble?
- Are there any roads or bridges in need of maintenance?
- What happens when a bridge between cities is broken?
- What can be done to repair the bridge?

Cities that are cut off from other cities won't thrive. Similarly, cities that are completely dependent on another city won't thrive. That's why it's important to develop interdependence in children rather than independence or dependence. Kids must learn that a maturing life is about creating, maintaining, and repairing connections between cities as their own cities continually grow and develop into the cities God designed them to be.

When a city doesn't develop quite like God intended it to develop, the surrounding cities miss out just as much as the city that was stunted in its growth. However, delays and difficulties are part of the process of growth and development for every city. Each city needs to be in constant communication with the Master Architect, Designer, and Builder as it adapts to the ever-changing and ever-challenging process of city, road, and highway development and maintenance.

I remember plenty of times I've had to repair bridges and highways with my family. One time in particular stands out. I had a lot on my plate that day. There was a project I was struggling to finish and a deadline I was trying to meet. There were multiple things converging at once. The situation felt like a Dallas freeway—chaotic and overwhelming. The pressure was pretty intense. By the time I got home, I felt as though my brain was going to explode. I was thinking about everything I needed to get done, and I wanted to spend some quiet time with my family. Yet, I walked in the door with a backpack full of paperwork still calling for attention. That's when Lexi and I intersected.

Lexi wanted us to connect. She was ready to visit my city and wanted me to visit her city. My daughter, Lexi, can get instantaneously hyper—in a good way, of course! She's warm, relational, talkative, outgoing, enthusiastic, and full of energy. Her exuberance, combined with her love of singing, can be incredible—but can also be somewhat overwhelming when your sensory networks aren't ready for it. On this particular evening, it was obvious that she was excited about something. Even out in the driveway I had heard her beautiful voice singing! Before I had a chance to put my things down, she ran up, hugged me like a boa constrictor around my waist, and in the process also squeezed my intestines and spleen. She told me all about her day and started launching a barrage of questions my way.

At the same time, my wife was trying to talk to me, while my son chimed in for my attention. This is when my brain experienced "a moment." Rush hour traffic was happening in all of the major connections to my city.

"Stop!" I said sternly, as I sent a search team out for my brain. Almost immediately Lexi's face changed. She stepped back. I stopped all traffic coming in and out of our cities. In an instant, I could see Lexi felt disconnected and hurt. I realized that I had not handled that moment well. Lexi didn't know what had been happening in my city all day. I was having a difficult time adapting to the many demands on me, and as Lexi and I intersected, she quickly found out I was not ready for any more traffic.

I know that I'm not unique in this build-build-build-and-pop moment. Every day parents face sleep deprivation, school meetings, schedules, work, kids lacking self-control, illness, messes, diaper changes, marriage, friendships, questions—the list could go on and on. Sometimes we do it right, and sometimes we don't. Parenting truly is a journey toward sanctification and learning to be contributors, however imperfect, in our children's lives.

PARENTAL STRESS

It's fascinating to me that at each stage of parenting, parents have common stresses. Before birth, stress is caused by the preparation—earning as much as possible, preparing a room for an infant, and knowing that your lives will be changed forever. After birth, stress is caused by sleep deprivation, diapers, and caring for a child who is completely dependent on you for survival. Often there are financial, time, and energy stresses during this stage of parenting, especially if you have more than one child.

A couple of years later, stress is caused by the well-known terrible twos and threes. A child's behaviors, opinions, and independence that seem to come out of nowhere make this a stressful time for parents.

At the preschool age, stress is caused by the pressure that parents may not be exposing their child to enough books, words, experiences, or educational toys. Comparisons between parents are thick. Parents may not admit it, but if we could see their thought bubbles, we would find a flood of insecurities, comparisons, and judgments. A lack of energy, finances, and time continue to add stress.

At kindergarten, stress is caused by emerging friendships, endless comparisons, and kids spending more time at school. For many parents, it is a big stress for a child to be at home less and to spend more time at school and with peers. Behavior issues, household finances, time crunches, and a lack of energy can also add to stress. This is a critical age for kids to learn self-control. Many kids will need very focused help in this area.

During the elementary-school years, parental stress is caused by chores, grades, vacations, and day-to-day demands.

During the preteen years, stress is caused by the anticipation of and preparation for adolescence. The body begins to change, and puberty begins to emerge. The brain is preparing for some big changes that will affect growth, mood, and responses. This changes the child's behavior in ways that are difficult for parents to adjust to.

During the teen years, stress is caused by the influence of peers on a child's decision making as well as by time demands and growing independence. The teen brain is at its most vulnerable because it's so responsive to rewards, risks, and new things or experiences. The teen years offer an incredible time for learning. All of these changes can present a lot of challenges for parents as they help a teen grow toward adulthood.

This is a quick and very general list, but you get the point. The challenges are unpredictable and unique to each child and to each family. We must adapt as our kids grow and change. This may cause stress, but it also brings great opportunity and great reward.

One thing I love about parenting is that as we influence our kids, they also influence us. For example, kids are wired for engagement from the time they are infants. They seek their parents' faces, voices, and attention and draw their mom or dad in toward a smile, tickle, touch, or play for however long they can keep their parent engaged. If a parent is too stressed out or distracted, he or she may miss out on these cues toward connection and attachment.

Unfortunately, the parent will also miss out on the oxytocin release that can come from emotional connection. Oxytocin is a bonding hormone that our body secretes to build attachment and foster feelings of safety, security, and connection with others. It also helps calm down stress in our limbic system. God created our bodies to respond to connectedness.

Oxytocin is released when the body experiences a safe and soothing touch, like a hug, soft touches on the arms or face, or even a massage. In our home, growing up as a Latino, I was used to touch. There were lots of hugs and *cosquillitas*, which are soothing tickles on the arm, face, back, or head. When my mom would give me *cosquillitas* at church, I would feel calm, safe, and relaxed. I have continued the tradition of *cosquillitas* with my kids, and they love it. I can easily see that this has created a greater bond through the release of oxytocin. Safe and loving touch is an essential component to attachment. I have noticed that I also feel calmer and more relaxed when I am giving my kids *cosquillitas*. We get a mutual stress-reducing benefit even though I'm the one giving them *cosquillitas*.

Other ways in which oxytocin can be released include hearing a loved one's voice, seeing his or her smile, and laughing together. Interestingly, stress reduces the production of oxytocin and the overall functioning of the oxytocin system. Additionally, when there is ongoing conflict in the home, oxytocin is also suppressed. As a result, there is less relational glue and fewer emotionally calming hormones flowing, which then increases disconnection, depression, frustration, and conflict.

God, in His incredible design, created oxytocin as a neuroprotective chemical for our brain. He designed the human body to have amazing benefits from healthy connections with others through touch, smiles, hugs, encouraging words, familiarity, *cosquillitas*, attention, and relationship.

The potential sources of parental stress are almost end-less. On top of their own personal, relational, professional, financial, spiritual, emotional, and material needs, mothers and fathers need to think about protecting and providing for their kids. What's more, they have to meet this incred-ible challenge in the context of an ever-shifting culture that lacks an understanding of the importance of a relationship with God.

Thanks to persuasive technology, which is designed to persuade its users to change their attitudes or change their behaviors, parents have even more challenges as they raise their children. Technology and other entertainment offer an ongoing barrage of new things parents need to monitor, dis-cuss, and limit. In fact, a new term introduced to our culture is *technoference*, which refers to the interference of technology in relationships. Parents consistently say that their biggest challenges in parenting are teaching their kids about biblical sexuality, limiting entertainment and technology, and man-aging different personalities in the home. These present addi-tional challenges to getting the oxytocin benefits of genuinely connected, face-to-face interaction.

"WE HAVE MET THE ENEMY, AND HE IS US"

How many of us fall prey to the belief that life must be easy, without any inconveniences, discomfort, or pain? I would venture to guess that most of us want things to go the way we want them to go, and we want everything to turn out just right and safely, especially for our children. For years I have prayed, "Lord, keep us safe, keep my family safe," but I am learning that as contributors, God wants us to be steadfast followers and believers, not just safe ones. In our attempts to protect our children, we often expend great effort trying to control things that we can't control.

Adults find plenty of big things to be stressed about: health care, mass shootings, money, the economy, family relationships, relationships in general, family responsibilities, and the speed and pace of modern life. That's just part of the story, of course. There are hundreds of smaller, more personal factors that also have to be taken into account. What's more, the longer we live and the more our brains experience, the faster time seems to move. This, too, increases our sense of being under pressure. The faster the wheel turns, the more desperate our desire to find a way off the merry-go-round, and sometimes we just feel like sleeping, screaming, or crying.

People look for relief in many different ways. Some of us use entertainment or technology. Some of us become easily angered or irritable. Some of us stop caring and disconnect from relationships. Others slip into anxiety or fatigue or try to find a way out through addictive behaviors or some other form of escapism. In every instance, the external conditions, whatever they may be, are allowed to push the brain "over the edge" and into a place where it becomes reactive.

When we're operating in a reactive mode, we tend to blame our circumstances. We say, "I'm worried because I don't have enough money to pay my bills" or "I'm angry because Johnny failed his math test." What we don't realize is that it's not the situation but our interpretation of the situation that's causing the problem. The trigger is on the inside, not the outside. The power to flip the switch and purposefully choose how we respond lies completely in our own hands.

Stress is primarily the result of our interpretation of a given situation. We look around, take in the details of our surroundings, and decide what we think is going on. We jump ahead and judge the situation as good or bad instead of observing what is happening and choosing how to respond. For example, when my family is late in leaving for vacation, many emotions and thoughts can arise in my mind. I would love to leave as early as possible, but it rarely goes as planned. I could interpret our lateness as bad by assuming that those few hours we are late are critical to making the vacation fun. However, I could instead choose to see the extra preparation hours as an opportunity to model patience, love, and cooperation. I can respond by making the preparation time fun and by seeing that time as a part of our vacation time together. I can guarantee you that my response makes a big difference in how the family vacation begins emotionally for all of us.

Moms and dads have a lot of power in setting the tone in the home and in everyday moments. How my wife and I choose to respond to every situation has a ripple effect that runs through everyone in our home.

Scripture can get the mind where it needs to be regardless of the circumstances. Look at Romans 5:3-5:

Not only that, but we rejoice in our sufferings, knowing
that suffering produces endurance, and endurance produces
character, and character produces hope, and hope does not
put us to shame, because God's love has been poured into
our hearts through the Holy Spirit who has been given to us.

The apostle Paul faced many stress-inducing circumstances during the course of his remarkable ministry. He faced opposition, prison, problems in the churches, and differences of personality with people in ministry with him. It became excruciatingly difficult for him along the way, but he learned to manage his thinking in order to handle these challenges. He knew the challenges of the mind. Consider what he wrote:

And the peace of God, which surpasses all understanding,
will guard your hearts and your minds in Christ Jesus. Finally,
brothers, whatever is true, whatever is honorable, whatever
is just, whatever is pure, whatever is lovely, whatever is
commendable, if there is any excellence, if there is anything
worthy of praise, think about these things. (Philippians 4:7-8)

Not that I am speaking of being in need, for I have learned
in whatever situation I am to be content. I know how to be
brought low, and I know how to abound. In any and every
circumstance, I have learned the secret of facing plenty and
hunger, abundance and need. I can do all things through
him who strengthens me. (Philippians 4:11-13)

These Scripture passages give us a glimpse into the strategies Paul used to take control of his thoughts and to adapt to the situations he faced in a way that was beneficial to him and honoring to God. These Scriptures show us what it means to be an adaptable Christian.

As Christians, we also have the miraculous and amazing reality of the Holy Spirit living and working through us. This reality makes us adaptable to circumstances through prayer, trust, and alignment with our heavenly Father. Prayer can help the mind realign with God. Prayer is also a way for multiple minds to be united toward a common desire. It brings hope and peace to an often chaotic brain.

Through relationship with the Holy Spirit and the healthy directing and redirecting of the mind, our own spiritual being is built on a solid foundation and we are able to grow and mature. This is what helps us adapt to the ever-changing circumstances of life and parenting.

It is critical that our children learn to have a relationship with God rather than seeing God as a distant being waiting to lay down rules and punishments. But if children learn, instead, to align their minds with the mind of Christ, they will learn to see life, circumstances, and relationships differently. They will be able to see a loving God, the sacredness of marriage, the benefits of family, and the transforming role of parenting. Psalm 119 provides an incredibly solid understanding of God's laws and statutes as beneficial to guiding the mind. The psalmist mentions his intention to meditate on God's precepts, works, and promises six times in Psalm 119.

THIS IS YOUR BRAIN ON STRESS

When you're under stress, your body secretes a powerful hormone called cortisol, which, like many beneficial drugs, can have harmful effects in large doses. Chronic stress depletes the body of neurotransmitters, leading to an increase in anxiety and depression. It can also trigger the onset of psychophysical symptoms such as memory loss, irritability, ulcers, and irritable bowel syndrome—conditions with which many overtired parents are all too familiar.

All of this can do significant damage to your body, mind, and soul. It can also hurt the people around you and introduce conflict into family relationships. Stress has a ripple effect. When parents react, it's easy for children to misinterpret. This, in turn, creates stress in their young hearts and minds.

I recall all too well how my own stress level affected my son, Alex, when he was only four years old. Parents often assume that toddlers are oblivious to what's going on in the adult world. They aren't. In the early days of my marriage, I struggled to adapt to the challenges of working, counseling, raising a child, and relating to a spouse. Though he couldn't have expressed it in words, Alex could see what was happening to me.

One night at dinner, when my brain was completely "locked up" in my own perceptions of my problems, he suddenly got down from his chair, grabbed a toy screwdriver, and came over to where I was sitting. "Daddy broken," he said, holding the plastic screwdriver to my side. It was as if God was speaking to me through my little boy. Tears came

INFO

Past Performance Does Not Equal Future Results

God has wired us to learn, grow, and adapt. Wouldn't it be great if we always used past experiences carefully to make new and better decisions? In case you haven't noticed, human beings are smart but make lots of mistakes. Researchers are discovering that this may have a lot to do with our stress levels.

According to studies conducted by neurologists from the University of Iowa, New York University, and the California Institute of Technology, the frontopolar cortex of the brain helps us predict future events on the basis of past experiences.[1] In other words, it has the power to project an established pattern onto circumstances that haven't yet come to pass.

This region of the brain is what helps humans make the best possible decisions in unpredictable and unfamiliar environments. The brain gathers information from what is known and tries to figure out what could happen.

What a person has experienced, how the experiences were remembered, and what the experiences meant to that person are all filtered through a personality lens that is unique to each person. The person then interprets the current situation, and the brain uses shortcuts to respond quickly and efficiently. This leaves a lot of room for error.

The functions of the frontopolar cortex can be useful in some situations. But in others it can produce needless worry and stress. That's because we can draw conclusions that aren't based on what really happens but on what the brain has concocted as possibilities.

For example, a child may hit another child because he's tired, but he may be acting out because of anger or any one of a number of reasons, including stress, loneliness, or feeling rejected by the other children. The list of possibilities is long.

The parent may react to the hitting by assuming the worst about why the child is acting out based on the parent's past experience. However, it's best to correct the behavior and then intentionally explore why the child chose to hit someone. Adapt what you think about the event by connecting to the world in your child's mind. This takes time, energy, patience, and careful listening.

down my face as I looked at my son's innocent and loving face. My mind and his connected as I felt compassion and love for my son. My brain was renewed by God's transforming love, which snapped me out of my brain-lock and made it possible for my mind to reengage with my family. Thanks to God speaking to me through Alex, I was able to recognize the real source of my stress: the chaos in my brain. That was the first step toward taking control of my response.

FOUR KEY STRATEGIES

As in every other area of parenting, there is no perfect pathway to adaptability. I've already pointed out that certain personality types find it easier to manage stress than others. This is further complicated by the fact that personality is itself a kind of adaptation: It's basically your individual method or style of interacting with the world around you and the filter you use to interpret what is happening in and around you. While parents play a huge role in shaping the family environment, they are also shaped and molded by it themselves. But none of this should be taken to mean that we're helpless in the face of the stresses we face as parents. It simply suggests that adaptability, like every other aspect of parenting, is an art rather than a science.

There are four strategies you need to adopt if you want to develop as an adaptable parent.

1. Having a Flexible Mindset

Flexibility is the ability to see things from multiple perspectives. It's about leaving room for humor and imperfection in the midst of the pressures and disappointments of everyday life. This comes naturally to some people, not so much to others. But it's a skill that we all need to cultivate if we want to survive and thrive as parents in a world of adversity and unpredictability.

Flexibility requires an open mind and a willingness to dig deeper. This is important because there's always more than one side to every story as well as multiple ways to interpret any situation.

Let's say you catch your child in a lie. Just to complicate matters, let's also suppose that your child is defiant as well as untruthful. The easy thing to do—the inflexible thing—would be to focus on the dishonesty and the disrespect and to hand out some kind of punishment immediately. But flexibility—an openness to seeing things from multiple perspectives—might lead you to take a very different approach.

For instance, you might ask some questions about the circumstances that inspired the dishonesty. What might your child have seen, heard, or interpreted, whether from you or from someone else, that could possibly have influenced her to tell a lie? Is she struggling with a particular emotion—fear, anxiety, frustration, or anger—that might have played a role in shaping her behavior? If so, is there anything you can do to address that emotion and get to the root of the problem?

If your daughter is afraid of telling the truth because she thinks it will get her into trouble, it might be a good idea to ask, "Do you think feeling afraid of getting in trouble or losing your toy caused you to choose to lie? It makes sense that you would lie if that is how you see it. You don't want to get in trouble or lose a toy. I wouldn't either, but I want to have a great relationship with you, and I want you to have a great relationship with other people, so it is super important for you to learn to be honest no matter what. Dishonesty disconnects and creates distrust. If you're trying to protect yourself, do you think there might be a better way of going about it rather than lying?"

We have a couple of mottos in our house. Whenever it makes sense to, we ask ourselves, "Is there another way to look at this?" Whenever we face difficulties, we say, "There is always a solution." Having a flexible mindset makes a big difference in how we respond to what is happening and how we manage relationships.

2. Looking at the Bigger Picture

Stress and shortsightedness can cause a vicious cycle in our lives. On the one hand, shortsightedness causes stress. That's because when we focus too intently on our own problems, we tend to lose touch with the rest of the world. This has the effect of constricting our horizons, increasing emotional claustrophobia, and heightening our sense of helplessness.

On the other hand, stress causes shortsightedness. That's because stress has the effect of magnifying our difficulties and making them look bigger than they really are. Under its influence, problems swell to the point where we can no longer see beyond them.

Once you're in the loop of stress and shortsightedness, it can be hard to escape. One of the best ways to break free is to move our thoughts toward the bigger picture.

ACTIVITY

Exercise: Family Role Play

Here's a great way to broaden your perspective and understand the other members of your family. It's also good for breaking down barriers and generating lots of laughs! I call it the Family Role Play game, and this is how it works.

Get everyone in your family together and take turns switching roles and pretending to be one another in exaggerated ways. Your goals are to create laughter and connection and to gain insight about each other. Keep in mind that the kids need to be able to handle being funny yet respectful with the understanding that the exercise is intended to help the family grow closer. This shouldn't become an opportunity to make fun of a family member or to point out a flaw in a mean-spirited way. Use discernment as you consider using this exercise.

The key to the exercise is to imagine that the whole group is in some kind of interesting, unusual, funny, or stressful situation. For example, you're on a road trip, and the car has just broken down in the middle of nowhere. Then act out the thoughts, feelings, and reactions of the family member you've been assigned to impersonate as faithfully, accurately, and respectfully as you can. You'll be surprised to see other people's interpretations of your actions and behavior! When the role play is over, talk about what you've seen and heard. This will be a good opportunity for some genuine, heart-to-heart communication!

We were waiting to go swimming when my son and daughter decided to start the Family Role Play game. My daughter pretended to be me. She made it clear that I love to ask questions. She said with a serious tone and look, "Okay, kids, tell me what you're thinking about. What are your dreams? What have you been feeling?" She also decided to show my somewhat antsy side: "Guys, hurry and finish eating so we can go swimming together." I can't remember all of the other things she said in my place because we were laughing so hard at the truths we were lightheartedly revealing about each other. We had a great time, and it was helpful insight for me on how I come across to my wife and kids.

Seeing the bigger picture means cultivating our ability to pause and consider how we're interpreting what is happening and then seeing things from multiple perspectives. This requires stepping outside of ourselves.

Think about the analogy of cities and highways. Things look much different when you look at the road map than they do when you're actually in each city or on a highway. Picture yourself stepping back and looking at a road map of your family's cities and highways. What do you want and hope for each other's cities and roads? Is there too much going on in your city? Do you need to say no to a few things? What can you do to regain perspective? Your children need your mentoring along the way. Very little about what children do to misbehave is personal to you as a parent. Children are just responding to their experiences in life as they learn how to manage themselves.

It is helpful to hit the pause button long enough to get your bearings and think through your plan of action. I once counseled a mom who told me that she'd had enough. "It's all too much for me," she explained with a haggard look on her face. "I've got nothing left. I'm empty. Done. I don't want to be a mom anymore."

As she continued to visit my counseling office, one thing became clear to me: This mother didn't have any pause buttons in her life. She had forgotten how to stop and observe. She didn't know how to say no or to step off the treadmill and figure out how to take care of herself. As a result, she was overwhelmed by everyday life and, sadly, emotionally and mentally distracted when she was with her children.

As we talked, she agreed that pause buttons were crucial and would be helpful to figuring out what to do and where to go mentally and emotionally. She drew "pause" buttons that she posted around her house and in her car as reminders, and she was able use these moments of pause to observe what was happening, gain perspective, and consider what guidance her mind needed. She saw the benefit of learning what her children's cities looked like and how to build highways of connection with them. This mom made a point to consistently take time to pray, go for a quick walk, do some stretching, and find time to laugh. These things helped fill her emotional bucket, and as a result, she was able to listen more attentively to her children, respond to them, and be more patient with them. In other words, she learned to create peace in her mind while the outside world was chaotic.

This mom worked hard to understand herself and others. For example, when her daughter was misbehaving, instead of just reacting, she practiced noticing what might be happening in her daughter's life. She considered what might be contributing to her daughter's choices. She looked through her daughter's eyes with compassion and wonder, and she mentally stepped into her daughter's world.

She also learned to observe her own internal chaos when she wanted to say yes but the best thing to do was to say no. She realized that her mind had been tricked into the quicksand of wanting to please people. She was exhausting herself trying to gain love by saying yes to everyone and everything that was asked of her, which was not a sustainable or healthy way to find love and acceptance.

The Pause That Refreshes

Sometimes stress can be so intense that it causes us to forget. We forget appointments, meetings, house keys, where we parked our car—you name it! This suggests that one of the biggest challenges involved in "hitting the pause button" is simply remembering to do it! When things get too hectic and pressured, this little exercise will remind you to stop and take another look.

All you need are some sticky notes and a pen. On each sticky note, draw a circle to represent a button. In big letters, write the word *Pause* in the circle. Then post the notes in different locations around the house: the refrigerator, bathroom mirrors, doors, dresser drawers, cupboards, computer

She used the pause moments to visualize herself and her children visiting each other's cities and managing the various highways connecting them to one another. This was not an easy task! She learned that it was up to her to build what was needed in her city and in the highways connecting her city to other cities. She was also able to recognize the importance of stop signs in her city and on the highways to other cities. This is what it means to look at the bigger picture.

3. Having a Growth Mindset

A few years ago, Carol Dweck came out with an essential book (*Mindset: The New Psychology of Success*, Ballantine Books) describing two important mindsets: the growth mindset and the fixed mindset. In her book, she gives compelling evidence for the importance of having and instilling a growth mindset in our children. Having a growth mindset includes letting go of the pursuit of perfection. It involves making a willful decision to stop focusing on certain things that stymie you and shifting your attention to other things that allow for the possibility of progress. It involves managing attention, practicing patience, and consciously choosing which battles to fight and which thoughts to allow to dominate your mind. This is excruciatingly difficult!

I sometimes fall into a more fixed mindset in times of stress. This means I think I either have the skills to deal with the issue at hand or I don't. This keeps me from being able to see creative solutions and to allow myself space to experiment, change, and grow. A fixed mindset perceives oneself as static and unchanging. A fixed mindset will stunt your growth.

In contrast, a growth mindset sees life as an endless opportunity for change and growth. It leaves plenty of room for experimentation, failures, do-overs, resets, and restarts. In a growth mindset, grace toward self and others helps us adapt to human imperfections. The grace inherent in a growth mindset also helps you

screens—anyplace where you and your family members will see them. Let everybody know that they can "press" one of these "pause" buttons whenever they feel stress or chaos beginning to take control. It's a good way to stay mindful of the need to stop and reorient your viewpoint every once in a while.

Shoulds vs. Coulds

We often use the word *should* in our mind and in conversations because we would love to predict or control the future or other people; however, the word *could* is much more freeing. For example, if you think a vacation *should* go a certain way, you're bound to a particular expectation. And if the vacation doesn't meet that expectation, you're set up for disappointment or judgment. On the other hand, if you think of what the vacation *could* be like, the pressure is off and you have freedom and flexibility. It's okay if the vacation isn't perfect or is different from what you envisioned.

A common conflict, especially for dads, is the expectation that their sons or daughters *should* do well

maintain the perspective that raising kids is a journey of ups and downs.

Letting go of the ideal and moving toward growth as a child of God is freeing. God gives both parents and children many opportunities to grow. He never said parents were going to start with all of the necessary skills to be perfect parents. He consistently says to trust in Him and connect with Him along the journey.

Consider Joseph (see Matthew 1:18-25) and Mary (see Luke 1:26-38) when they received the unexpected news that Mary, a virgin, would miraculously conceive and bear the Savior of the world. They both did as the Lord's angel commanded and viewed the moment through the lens of a contributor. In fact, Mary said, "I am the servant of the Lord; let it be to me according to your word" (Luke 1:38). In their wildest dreams, they couldn't have foreseen that this was what God had for them. They both certainly had much more conventional ideas about their future together as husband and wife. However, they let go of how they thought things should be and pursued obedience to what God was saying. This required a close and intentional relationship with God. Their relationship to God provided them with the necessary discernment, acceptance, and patience to respond to the uncertainties and challenges they faced. Mary and Joseph let go of the belief that life would be easy and without inconveniences, discomforts, or challenges. This open, growth-oriented mindset, founded on trust in God, helped them adjust to the amazing life God planned for them.

in a sport. Substituting the word *could* is revolutionary for some parents. It provides them with the freedom to love their child regardless of how he or she performs. The word *could* allows parents to let go of what they cannot control.

4. Learning and Adjusting

The last essential ingredient of adaptability is a willingness to learn and adjust your parenting while you're on the job. Parenting is a challenge because children don't come with instruction manuals. Parents must adjust their strategies by using the knowledge they gain along the way and the wisdom they gain from what God is doing in them and in their children. Parents learn about their own personalities, their children's personalities, and the specific triggers that tend to bring out the positive and negative aspects of their personalities and parenting.

In parenting, you are shaping another human being while also being significantly shaped along the way. There are moments of growth for both you and your children. The ultimate challenge is that nobody on earth has ever raised your unique child before! Shelves of great parenting books have been written by hordes of eminent parenting experts, but not one of them is specific enough to speak directly to your son's or daughter's special and specific design. There's a sense in which the particular challenges you're facing are unique in the history of the world.

There's only one way to meet those challenges effectively: You've got to manage your mind and stay in the game, even when things aren't going right. Stick close to your child until you discover what makes him tick and what gets him moving in the direction of learning and growth. Study your child until you see patterns emerging. If in the process you sometimes feel like running, screaming, or throwing in the towel, remember that it's the twists and turns of life that keep us on our toes. Time, listening, and relationship are key ingredients to learning and adjusting.

Accept your own imperfections, seeing them as inevitable opportunities for growth. Lean on the Lord for strength and understanding. Take notes as you progress and learn from your mistakes. If you do this, not only will you succeed at your task, but I predict that you will also set the kind of personal example that will enable your children to grow spiritually. All you have to do is bring your imperfect self to the job and give everything you can give out of your imperfect best. You are, after all, the very best candidate for the job.

PRACTICAL TIPS FOR MANAGING STRESS

Now that you understand the four key ingredients of adaptability, we can finish this chapter with a few thoughts on simple stress management. As I said at the beginning of the chapter, stress is a given for all of us at every stage of our earthly existence, but especially during the parenting years. None of us can escape it, but we can all start practicing some basic strategies to help us handle it more efficiently.

Keep this fundamental principle in mind: Situations don't cause stress; perceptions do. I realize I've already made this point, but I think it's worth reiterating here. Stress is self-generated. It's not your leaky radiator or your son's report card that pushes you over the edge. It's your perception of the significance of a major car repair or a failing grade that gets the stress rising.

Similarly, it's not necessarily your hectic schedule that frazzles you. After all, some people seem to thrive when their calendars are maxed out. Instead, the frazzle may come from your perception that you should react to your schedule in a certain way ("Yikes! When will I ever have a chance to get some rest?"). It's the *should* that creates the stress.

You can relieve some stress by making an effort to see the situation from a different angle. For example, if you assume that it's your responsibility as a parent to ensure that your child

Stress Menu

Draw a stress continuum of 0 to 10 for yourself. Zero is having no stress—you might describe it as peacefully lying on a hammock by a beach with no demands. Ten is having major, catastrophic stress. Add the numbers 1 to 9 to the continuum and label each number with a word that describes something that you find stressful. These stress-inducers should escalate progressively from *hammock* to *disaster*.

Next, make a list of things that you could do for self-care in a time of stress. You can make a list of things that will not take much time and effort and a list of things that will take more time and effort. Keep adding to the menu as you think of new things. You can access this stress

stays happy all the time, you'll respond with stress every time you suspect your child is unhappy. If you shift your perspective and remind yourself that you aren't in charge of your child's happiness, you can rid yourself of that burden fairly easily. It's simply a matter of altering your viewpoint.

It can also be helpful to understand that emotions help us experience moments and are not necessarily bad. For example, sadness helps us grieve and shows that something was lost. Anger helps us understand what we strongly dislike. Emotions make sense of the context of our situation and our thoughts.

There are at least four things you can do to prepare yourself when you know that life is about to hit you with a barrage of potentially stress-producing demands.

Pray

When family circumstances seem overwhelming and your mind is in chaos, prayer is the believer's indispensable reset button. It's the very best way to get back to basics and regain your grasp on the bigger picture. Prayer has helped me remember that the window of influence as a parent to my children is brief and that I need to make each day count.

Sleep

Consistent and adequate sleep is an essential ingredient to succeeding as a parent and in managing stress. Sleep deprivation is quite common among parents. A recent study suggests that REM sleep is associated with mental flexibility as well as greater problem-solving and creative abilities.[2] Our brains need sleep to prepare for the next day. The way I love to picture the need for sleep is to picture each day as a fun gathering. My brain needs time to clean up from today's fun gathering and to organize and prepare for the next day's gathering. If I don't give my brain enough time through sleep to clean up, organize, and prepare, the event will be a mess the following day.

menu whenever you notice your stress level climbing.

You can do this exercise as a family to learn each other's stress levels and inducers as well as what each of you finds helpful for bringing your stress level down. Encourage one another to use the list of self-care activities. It is difficult to remember to use healthy stress reducers when we are in the middle of stress. It is as if we go on auto-survival mode.

Moderation

Use wisdom and moderation in your consumption. There's a strong connection between the brain and what we consume physically (food), emotionally (in our relationships), and mentally (entertainment, technology, news). This means that what we consume is vital not only to physical health but also to good emotional and mental health. Placing safeguards in these areas of your life can give you the health you need to respond well to stress. What are you consuming physically, mentally, relationally, emotionally, and spiritually?

Exercise

Exercise helps maintain the functions of your brain, your nervous system, your digestive tract, and your heart and blood vessels. I can tell you from years as a counselor that parents who made the time for exercise were less stressed, more engaged and more confident, and generally sported a more open and wise mind in parenting. Exercise is also a great way to help your mind let some things go and to allow for a helpful endorphin release for your brain.

TRUST—GOD WITH US

God has pledged to stand beside us and give us the strength and wisdom we need as we courageously face the difficulties and uncertainties of raising kids and living life in this world.

Let these encouraging passages take root in your mind as

you consider how you can manage your mind and adapt to the ever-changing circumstances of raising children.

You keep him in perfect peace whose mind is stayed on you, because he trusts in you. (Isaiah 26:3)

I have said these things to you, that in me you may have peace. In the world you will have tribulation. But take heart; I have overcome the world. (John 16:33)

And let the peace of Christ rule in your hearts, to which indeed you were called in one body. And be thankful. (Colossians 3:15)

ADAPTABILITY

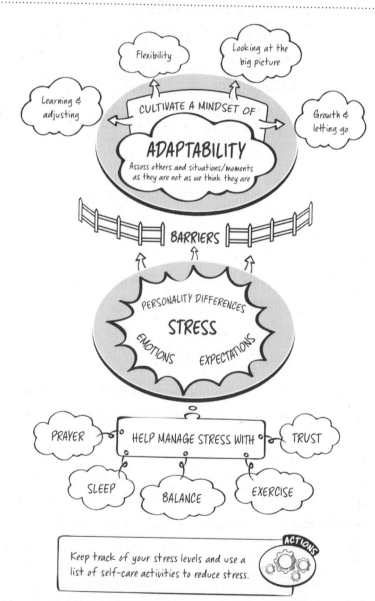

Flexibility

Looking at the big picture

Learning & adjusting

CULTIVATE A MINDSET OF

Growth & letting go

ADAPTABILITY

Assess others and situations/moments as they are not as we think they are

BARRIERS

PERSONALITY DIFFERENCES

STRESS

EMOTIONS   EXPECTATIONS

PRAYER   HELP MANAGE STRESS WITH   TRUST

SLEEP   BALANCE   EXERCISE

ACTIONS

Keep track of your stress levels and use a list of self-care activities to reduce stress.

CHAPTER 3

RESPECT

Respect begins with this attitude: I acknowledge that you are a creature of extreme worth.

–GARY CHAPMAN

Show proper respect to everyone, love the family of believers, fear God, honor the emperor.

–1 PETER 2:17, NIV

I WAS COACHING MY SON and six other boys in a middle-school basketball tournament. We were playing a team we had played before, and a few of the boys mentioned their annoyance and frustration with a player on the opposing team.

I understood their point of view. This boy was a good basketball player, but he was also arrogant, manipulative, and argumentative. He would say things to players on our team under his breath and then smile at the referees and try to joke with them. He would do things to our players while the refs weren't watching.

His respect was conditional. He respected whoever could provide what he wanted. As the game progressed and the score grew close, he began complaining and arguing with the refs, his coach, his teammates, and the players on my team. Meanwhile, in the stands, a husband and wife, along with their adult daughter and her boyfriend or husband, launched a verbal assault on one particular referee that escalated throughout the game.

Finally, in the fourth quarter, the ref stopped the game. The dad and mom stormed the court and got in the referee's face, screaming obscenities for all to hear. The director of the tournament came over and told them they needed to leave the gym or he would call the police. They continued their all-out tantrum for all the players to see.

When the parents finally started making their way to the door, their daughter and the young man who was with her approached the referee and started yelling at him. My son and his teammates looked scared and confused. Eventually, the tournament director had to call the police, who met the disruptive family members at the door when they finally exited the building. The game was stopped for several minutes during the outburst.

Guess whose parents it was who made such a scene? It was the family of the boy my players had complained about during the game. The boy was simply mirroring the disrespectful attitude and behavior he had learned from his family. Yes, he was responsible for his own behavior, but what we observed in his family explained a lot about his behavior.

Respecting others means seeing the value of people and treating them in accordance with that value. However, in sports, school, and other activities involving performance or stress, we can quickly get caught up in pursuing our own objectives and forget to actively respect others with our words and our actions.

WITH RESPECT

Our commitment to respecting others gets tested every day. Consider the slow cashier at the grocery store who doesn't seem to care that you're in a hurry or the restaurant server who can't seem to get your order right. What do you say about these people? How do your actions show your attitude toward them? Your kids are always watching and learning from your words and your actions. Your kids are taking their cues from you on how to treat others. What words, actions, and attitudes of yours might they mirror in their own dealings with others?

God's Word has a lot to say about respect. Genesis 1:27 lays the groundwork for respect by pointing out that every person is made in the image of God. In Philippians 2:1-8, the apostle Paul offers a mini tutorial on respect. His main emphasis is humility, which is the key ingredient of respect.

For the purposes of this book, we're going to focus on five areas in which respect can be cultivated and demonstrated: what we think, where we look, how we pay attention and listen, what we say, and what we do.

WHAT WE THINK

An average person has about fifty thousand thoughts a day. Where do they all go? My thoughts can go in all kinds of directions depending on my emotions, my stress level, my interests, and any number of other factors. My ability to purposefully direct the tens of thousands of thoughts that pass through my brain on a daily basis will go a long way toward developing a God-honoring respect for others. Second Corinthians 10:5 tells us to take every thought captive in order to make it obedient to Christ. Philippians 4:4-9 gives us some extremely useful guidelines for our thoughts:

> Rejoice in the Lord always; again I will say, rejoice. Let your reasonableness be known to everyone. The Lord is at hand; do not be anxious about anything, but in everything by prayer and supplication with thanksgiving let your requests be made known to God. And the peace of God, which surpasses all understanding, will guard your hearts and your minds in Christ Jesus. Finally, brothers, whatever is true, whatever is honorable, whatever is just, whatever is pure, whatever is lovely, whatever is commendable, if there is any excellence, if there is anything worthy of praise, think about these things. What you have learned and received and heard and seen in me—practice these things, and the God of peace will be with you.

I once wrote Philippians 4:8 on a card as a template to guide my thinking about my wife. It was a great exercise that I adopted during a season when my wife and I attended marriage counseling. It helped train my attention toward lovely, commendable, pure, honorable, just, and true things in my wife. Research supports the fact that the quality of the parents' relationship has a direct impact on the children's behaviors and emotions.[1] The more positive the marriage relationship, the more positive the child's development and behaviors. In other words, the way I treat my wife will have a direct influence on my children. My kids are watching and learning, whether they're writing notes or not. They begin to mirror what they see.

The city-and-road-construction analogy is helpful in visualizing respect. When the two metropolises (the parents) are thriving, the smaller surrounding cities (the children) thrive. I was on a basketball missions trip to Guatemala when our coach began to share how his marriage almost ended after two years. The coach recalled a mindset he was told to adopt by a mentor. This mindset transformed his marriage. He said he had adopted the question, "What is one thing I can do for my wife today

Mirror Neurons

As children grow, they do, say, feel, and think what they see others doing, saying, feeling, and thinking. This mirroring behavior is a strategy our brains use, with the help of the mirror neuron network, to help us learn, develop, and connect with others.

The mirror neuron network enables us to experience what another person is experiencing. It helps fuel empathy. For example, if a child watches someone get a hug, his or her brain sends signals similar to those it would send if he or she were getting a hug as well. If kids watch videos of other people shooting free throws, their brain rehearses what is being watched. It is as if the brain is experiencing what is being watched, so the person is actually mentally processing what he or she sees. This inevitably affects human behavior.

Have you ever noticed your son or daughter doing something you, your spouse, or his or her sibling do? Have you ever noticed yourself doing something your mom, dad, siblings, or other influential people in your life have done? While this can be good when a person is exposed to positive influences, this can be disconcerting when a person is exposed to negative influences, such as sexual, violent, vulgar, or defiant language or behavior. I have met several embarrassed parents whose toddlers have mirrored offensive language they heard from their parents in the home.

What you see in your kids, both good and bad, has you sprinkled in it as well. Take this as an opportunity for grace and growth.

Mirror neurons have all kinds of implications when you consider the messaging kids experience from music, videos, peers, and culture. Our kids are truly watching and learning.

to make her day better?" Small or big, he challenged himself to do something for his wife to help her know that she is important to him.

This coach modeled for us the importance of the marriage relationship and maintaining the emotional and relational highways between the two metropolises. As the two large cities (the parents) care about each other, listen to each other, and serve one another, they build stronger roads and bridges to help deal with difficult moments. When there is disrespect, conflict, and disconnection between the two larger cities, the smaller cities may experience roadblocks in their connections within the family. This can adversely affect the growth and development of the smaller cities.

Often kids become the focal point of parents' lives, and parents neglect to maintain the highways and bridges between themselves. Children in these kid-centric homes do not get the benefit of learning how to:

- respond to disappointment
- respond to the word *no*
- manage impatient feelings
- respect and understand limits and boundaries
- work toward goals with self-discipline
- maintain relationships
- serve others
- understand and respect others' ideas, wishes, and thoughts

Kids in kid-centric homes develop habits of thinking and behaving that lead them to be self-centered and chaotic—they don't develop a healthy interdependence.

In addition to maintaining their relationship to each other, there are a few basic things parents can do to foster respect in the way all family members think about one another.

Remembering

Remembering and being present for the important events and dates in our children's lives is an essential way to show respect. Being remembered feels like being known, being acknowledged, and being valued. Again, it's a matter of managing and training the many thoughts running through your mind. Keeping track of events and dates in other people's lives isn't easy, but it's worth the effort. Important events and dates can be written down on sticky notes, calendars, journals, notebooks, computers, or smartphones.

People feel valued and respected when aspects of their lives are known and remembered.

Being Present

Our kids notice when we are distracted, and it makes them feel unimportant. Taking time to pause your own thoughts in order to enter your children's worlds shows them that you place a high value and importance on them.

When my daughter was much younger, she thought I could read her mind. I would say, "Let me look deep into your eyes," and she would just stare into my eyes and ask, "What do you see?"

Then I would say, "I can see that you want . . ." or "I think you really wish . . ."

The fact was that I tried to make sense of what was happening in her mental world in that particular moment in time. What was she seeing and what might she really want? I would think about what she had been talking about and pay attention to the context of what was going on in her life in order to "read her mind" and complete the sentence. She loved that I would really try hard to know what was in her mind.

Being present in the moment and really paying attention to our children is so important. I picture the present as a true *present*, a gift. But if the gift isn't unwrapped and experienced, it's gone forever. These moments are so transitory, and yet the influence of these moments is profound and eternal. How do I spend my attention?

Renewing of the Mind

Remember that respect begins in the mind. Our emotions, which begin in the mind, can quickly get us off track. Our emotions can change how we interpret events and how we understand others. What is your attitude toward others? Do you see others as valuable simply because they are made in the image of God? When we are frustrated and annoyed with others, we can tend to forget their worth and see them with a mindset of disrespect. This is when we need to renew our minds.

Romans 12:2 says, "Do not be conformed to this world, but be transformed by the renewal of your mind, that by testing you may discern what is the will of God, what is good and acceptable and perfect." It is essential that we renew our minds in preparation for teaching, discipling, guiding, and mentoring our children. Not only will this help us be better in our parenting, it's also an opportunity to model this important biblical practice for our children.

Prayer is like a shower for the mind, and the Word of God is like water on a thirsty day for the mind. Get some rest, some space, and some refreshment through prayer and Scripture, so that your mind is ready to respond (instead of react) to the many twists and turns kids can bring into your life. I've noticed that when I'm tired and stressed and haven't gotten much time to pray or renew my mind with the Word of God, my mind can become chaotic, distracted, and impatient much faster.

WHERE WE LOOK

A basic way to show respect is to look at a person when he or she is talking. This doesn't guarantee that our attention will be directed at the person, but it increases the chances. Focusing the spotlight of our gaze on someone helps us to also focus our attention.

Researchers from the Massachusetts Institute of Technology,[2] as well as other researchers,[3] have found that visual processing is our most powerful sensory input. In fact, around 50 percent of the brain's sensory processing network is dedicated to the visual sensory system. What we look at greatly affects us. Our kids learn a lot by what we choose to look at. Our eyes quickly reveal what draws our attention, what we value, and what we pursue. We can model respect by the way we look at commercials, technology, billboards, and magazine racks, as well as how we look at people. Wherever your eyes go, your body and its response follow.

I'll never forget attending a conference where Gary Thomas was teaching. He said that when he enters a room, he asks himself if his eyes are assaulting others or bringing the love of Jesus.

As parents, where we choose to look and how we look can give tremendous instruction to our kids about respect and can communicate what is truly important to us.

I see many distracted parents, especially with the growth of technology. Recently at a home-improvement store I noticed a mom who had her two young kids with her. One of the mom's children was asking lots of questions while the mom texted on her phone. When the child began asking about a cactus, the mom tried halfheartedly to explain. Her attention, though, was being pulled in more than one direction, so she wasn't quite able to explain it in a way that made any sense. It looked painful. You could see that her brain was being pulled in multiple directions and that she was tired.

This young daughter used several different strategies to get her mother's attention. She was clearly craving the spotlight. She wanted to feel important to her mother. She was throwing out some bids for her attention by pulling and saying "Mommy, Mommy" repeatedly and asking the same question over and over again. The mom, though, was distracted by her phone. Phones offer incredibly tempting diversions from the present moment. Multiple conversations can be happening without people physically being present. To an adult, this is a great way to efficiently deal with a number of issues all at the same time. However, what children may interpret is that their parents are more interested in their phones than they are in their children. Ouch!

Children make frequent bids for their parents' attention when they are young, but over time this situation reverses. Parents are the ones who make frequent bids for their older children's attention.

We are being trained to be multitaskers and multi-communicators by having phones everywhere we go, but we are sacrificing focused attention and depth of experience. We

Where We Point Our Eyes

Another aspect of where we look has to do with sexual respect. Scripture tells us that Job made a covenant with his eyes. Our kids learn a lot about us by where we look. What captures our attention? Where do we choose to focus?

When my son was eight years old, we were walking in the mall. As we approached Victoria's Secret, I said, "Son, let's look to the right. There are some pictures I want you to learn to look away from, because they are not helpful for you as you become a man. I want you to learn to control your eyes." As I suspected, he gave the pictures a quick glance. I noticed him do this, so after we passed the area I asked him what he felt when he looked.

become conversation maintainers rather than conversation engagers.

There are a multitude of things that can shift a parent's attention away from children. How can your kids get your undivided attention?

Throughout the years I have counseled families, I have noticed the significant benefit of a designated hour for families to give one another their undivided attention. A lot can be learned and accomplished in an hour while attention is focused on the family dynamic and listening to one another.

HOW WE PAY ATTENTION AND LISTEN

We show respect for others when we pay attention and listen to them. However, attention has a cost. When I choose to pay focused attention to something or someone, I choose not to pay attention to other things or people because we can't truly focus our attention on more than one thing at a time.

Attention requires effort. That's

why when we're tired or stressed, we find it more difficult to focus our attention. Theories suggest that willpower can become depleted throughout the day, which can make it difficult to shift our attention toward setting limits on ourselves and/or others. I believe it takes self-awareness, practice, and maturity to learn how to manage depleting willpower.[4]

Attention is all-encompassing. My children feel important when they know that my mind, eyes, ears, hands, and mouth are "all in" on the conversation I'm having with them. This is hard! There tend to be a lot of things running through my mind at any given time.

Children want our genuine attention, and not an appeasing or halfhearted attention. I have seen kids light up when they get their parent's wholehearted gaze focused directly on them, wanting to connect. But children are very much aware when a parent's spotlight of attention is dim, hurried, or wandering. Children choose not to share as

My son said he felt "tinglies." I told him that was normal and that the pictures are tempting and designed to get our attention. "They are trying to sell something," I told him. "In this case, underwear." We talked about guarding his eyes as a way of respecting his future wife. In my counseling practice it is evident from working with males that training the eyes where to go and how to look takes a lot of work and intentionality. It is never too early to begin teaching this lesson.

much in conversation as they would have had the parent's spotlight of attention been bright and focused.

In any relationship, attention and respect flow back and forth between parties. An illustration I like to use with families I counsel is "trains of thought." Everyone has a train of thought running and sometimes trains collide. Unfortunately, there's only room on the tracks between your city and your child's city for one train at a time. Children often can't see that the parent's train is running at full speed and will run over whatever is in the way. In families, the trains of thought need to take turns on the tracks.

When I have lapses in attention with my children because my train is going too fast on the tracks, my kids have an opportunity to respect me by showing me grace. Then I have the opportunity to show them respect by pulling my train into the station and letting their train of thought have access to the tracks.

I recently asked my kids how they would rate me as a listener on a scale of 1 to 10, with 10 being perfect at listening and 1 being completely absent. Both of my kids said I am an 8, which shows they have lots of grace. There have been plenty of times when my mind has been distracted as I tried to listen. I'm pretty sure I got an 8 because they can see that I'm really trying hard to listen to them and that I truly want to truly know them.

Listening shows that a person cares—and, as my children demonstrate to me so often, grace that is offered when someone doesn't listen also shows that a person cares. I have to confess that I've been caught not listening to my kids, and I know you have too. I hate to admit this, but I've also sometimes not listened well as a spouse, friend, or counselor. I have also been on the receiving end of not being listened to on many, many occasions. Have you ever been talking to someone and had to start over—or found that the person completely disregarded what you said or didn't seem interested in what you had to say? It doesn't feel good at all! You don't feel as though you are important to the other person.

I recently picked up my daughter from school. I could tell that she was excited from the moment she jumped into the car. She sits right behind me in the car, so I can see her in the rear-view mirror. She was smiling and ready to flood me with words.

"How was your day?" I asked.

This ordinary question opened up the verbal floodgates! The problem was that my brain wasn't ready for the flood. I was still trying to resolve another issue in my mind.

My daughter finished and waited for a response from me. I was trying to process her final words in order to say something. Anything. (C'mon, I know you've been guilty of this too.) She knew I had, at most, half listened.

I could see the disappointment and frustration in her face. "I'm sorry," I said. "My train of thought was not ready for your train of thought."

"What?" she said with a slight, nervous chuckle. "I can't believe you didn't listen to me!" She wasn't mad. She was hurt. She didn't feel valued by me.

I followed up with, "I completely missed your exciting train. Mine had business stuff and yours had much more exciting things in it. I wish I would've hopped out of mine and jumped into your fun train of thought. Can we try again? I'm at the train station waiting for your train to pick me up. I just bought my ticket and I'm ready to go. When do you think the train will be coming back around to pick me up?"

She laughed. We were able to use humor and imagination to reconnect. She was able to forgive me and give me another chance to experience her train of thought.

My daughter had clearly felt disrespected. She also felt that she was unimportant to me in that moment, which wasn't true; I was just distracted by my own thoughts. The important takeaway from this story is the need to respectfully acknowledge when you could've listened but didn't. Listening shows others that they are important to you. You are showing them respect for what they have to say. It takes shifting your thoughts to allow for pictures to be formed in your mind.

Our kids need to understand that they sometimes have to patiently wait until we're ready to attentively listen. It's okay to tell them they need to wait. It is important to help them understand that you want to be able to fully listen. You are modeling how to respect with ears and mind joined together. This helps align the "spotlight" of our minds.

When you use the words "What I hear you saying is . . ." you are communicating respect and honing your focus. You are communicating that you truly want to get the picture that their words are trying to create. Listening involves knowing. Take time to absorb what is being said. Kids can tell when you're interested and when you're distracted. Giving them full eye contact can send the message that they are important to you. Eyes communicate a lot. If you move your inner world toward calmness and being present, you are more likely to tap into your intuition and enter their world with wisdom. In my counseling practice and in my personal life, listening is a big one. Feeling heard, listened to, and known creates the sense of being loved by someone. It demonstrates that the other person cares and wants relationship.

WHAT WE SAY

Respect provides the maturity needed to facilitate communication. The parents I told you about at the beginning of this chapter had not yet learned the maturity of self-control in regard to their words. They lacked the wisdom to let basketball be a game and they lacked the vision to teach their son to be respectful with his words. They aren't bad parents, but their emotions got them way off track.

Your kids learn a lot about life through what you say. You provide the narration to their experience of the world. What you say can build, connect, and destroy—sometimes within the same sentence or paragraph.

Patience and Self-Control

Many arguments in the home involve a lack of respect. It's inevitable because we are human. Several years ago, a grandfather and his grandson came to me for counseling. The grandfather, who had custodial care of the boy, wanted the best for his grandson. He wanted him to get good grades,

Stop-Sign Exercise

All conversations work like an intersection in traffic. Vehicles must stop at the intersection and take turns, or there will be a collision in the middle of the intersection. In the same way, people in conversation must stop and take turns to avoid a crash! This exercise can help your family develop awareness in listening to one another and taking turns contributing to conversation. Learning the art of give-and-take in conversation helps children learn to respect others.

Explain to your children how a traffic intersection works. Explain that when you have a conversation, you must stop and wait your turn just as cars take turns in traffic, and you must listen respectfully while the other person is talking.

You may want to make a paper stop sign that you can use to practice taking turns in conversation. Just remember not to use the stop sign to tell the other person to stop talking so that you can talk! Instead, after you take your turn in conversation, hold the stop sign yourself and indicate in polite, traffic-officer style that it's the other person's turn to talk. When that person is done talking, give him or her the stop sign to hold on to while you take up the conversation again.

When someone is speaking and a family member interrupts, the interrupted person can say, "I was in the intersection talking, and you came and collided with my car."

When you are in a conversation with another person or in a group, teach your child how to show you that he or she is at the intersection waiting to speak to you. The signal could be touching your hand or your leg or standing right next to you. I have had to train myself to notice when my kids are in the intersection waiting for me. Find a way to let your child know that you are aware that he or she is at the intersection waiting for a turn to talk. I put my hand on my child's shoulder and look for a pause in the conversation to let him or her into the intersection.

The stop sign can also be used as a do-over for kids. When a child is disrespectful, you can hand him or her the paper stop sign and say, "You can try that again, but this time with respect." When my son and daughter were much younger, I remember telling them a couple of times, "What happened to respect? Did you drop her off somewhere? We need to find her, so you can try this again with respect." My kids looked at me a little puzzled at first but got the point over time.

make good choices, and do well in life. He didn't want him to turn out like the grandson's parents and was parenting the grandson out of fear. Whenever the grandson made poor decisions or disobeyed, the grandfather interpreted it through a lens of fear and perceived it as a personal attack. As a result, the grandfather would become impatient and verbally disrespect his grandson when they would get into conflict. He would then be surprised and angry when his grandson started mirroring his behaviors back to him.

I'll give you another example of disrespectful conversation. I was in line at an amusement park with my son, waiting to get on a roller coaster, when I saw a boy in his early teens confused about where to go because he'd forgotten to get his things from the cubby after the ride. His dad proceeded to slap him upside the head and publicly ridicule him. You could see outwardly that his son was grappling with shame, anger, and a hardening of his heart toward his dad.

How would your kids say you talk to them? How would they say you talk to your spouse and to other people?

Do you talk disrespectfully about other people? How about when you're driving? Are you able to have patience with other drivers? I'll be the first to say that I have to practice awareness of how I speak about others, especially when I have felt frustrated with a coworker, extended family member, or rude stranger.

Verbal Culture

Each family develops their own culture within the larger overall culture. In a research study published in the *Journal of Family*

Psychology, researchers looked at the concept of respect within African American, Latino, and European American families. What they found is that African American and Latino homes placed higher emphasis on respect in the home than did the European American homes. This resulted in more respect for parental authority in the home. The researchers also found less conflict in homes that had higher levels of discipline and communication regardless of cultural background.[5]

Making respectful speech a constant rhythm in your life is quite a challenge. It's like working out. You don't ever arrive; it's a continuous process. There have been times when I've caught myself talking negatively about someone else with my kids. But I've learned that there are plenty of critics in our lives and not enough encouragers. I would rather be known by my kids as an encourager than as a critic.

According to the *Harvard Business Review*, top-performing teams give each other five positive comments for each criticism.[6] Criticisms tend to stick, while encouraging words need a little extra glue. Interestingly, researchers included sarcasm in with criticisms. While some find sarcasm to be funny, for others sarcasm is quite destructive.

Realize that each of your children may filter your words differently. Some personality types are more sensitive to criticism than others. While criticism is not all bad, it really does need to have purpose and be constructive to the person. One child may be motivated by constructive criticism, while another may need several encouraging words balanced with the constructive criticism.

Ask yourself these questions:

- How do others experience the words that I say?
- Does the person I'm speaking to feel that he or she is important to me?
- Do my kids wonder what I say about them when I'm not with them?

One day early in my career as a clinical social worker, I was thinking about how contagious people can be to others emotionally and mentally, especially when they are very negative or very positive. I really wanted the kids, teens, and families I was working with to understand how this could affect their family and how to work on more positive interactions in their relationships.

The more I worked with teens, the more I realized how certain odors affected others. Sometimes the teens knew they were making certain smells and sometimes they didn't. I also noticed that pizza is naturally inviting and that deodorant and essential oils can help the air quality of a room. The more I thought about these odors and aromas, an analogy began to form in my mind. I have counseled families to use the following ideas to help with communication regarding attitude and emotions in their homes.

Stink Bomb

Kids and teens love and remember this one. When someone comes into a room with a negative attitude, it is as if that person set off a stink bomb in the room. The person with a negative attitude is likely dealing with a number of difficult issues that make them feel bad. As these issues are expressed through the stink bomb of a negative attitude, everyone else has to deal with the stinky, negative attitude as it lingers in the room. What will they choose to do—cover their noses? Run out of the room? Or stand their ground and breathe it in?

The fact is that people have to adjust to what enters the mental and emotional airspace of a room. Some families using this illustration will tell a child, "Hey, I think you just lit a stink bomb in the room," and the child will most likely say, "No, I didn't." The parent must then explain that the bad attitude and negative emotions that the child is experiencing are invading other people's mental and emotional airspace. Having this conversation with your child can help him or her understand that our attitudes, as well as how we express our attitudes, affect others.

Pizza

When someone comes into the room with a positive attitude, it is as if that person entered the room with a pizza. Who doesn't like the smell of pizza? Everyone wants a slice. Bringing a pizza into the room is an opportunity for fellowship and fun—it's an instant party! This analogy is a great way to illustrate how a positive attitude can make people attractive in a way that makes others want to spend time with them. Let your kids know when they "bring a pizza into the room."

Body Odor

When someone comes in and is unaware of his or her negativity and rudeness, it is like having sweaty, smelly armpits. The person may not be aware, but the people around that person are very aware. Similarly, people can be negative, rude, or critical without knowing how they are affecting people around them.

Deodorant

When someone takes time for self-care in order to bring his or her best "me" to the room, it is as if they have put on deodorant for the day. I love the saying, "Taking care of yourself is part of your job." There will be plenty of times when life will try to produce a sweaty, smelly attitude, but self-care helps with strengthening self-control and patience. What can you do in the morning to prepare your mind for what may be coming that day? Are you managing stress well? If not, take some time to review the Adaptability chapter. How can you encourage your children to prepare themselves for the day? God provides a variety of "deodorants" in Colossians 3:12-15, Ephesians 5:1-2, and Ephesians 6:10-20.

Essential Oil Diffusers

When a family maintains a positive attitude even though a child is being negative, it is as if the family is a diffuser releasing essential oils to overcome the smell of the negative attitude. Several years ago, a mom came into my office and said, "You've been seeing a lot of teens today, haven't you?" I acknowledged that I had, and she went on to say,

"Well, I think you need a diffuser in your office to help with the various odors." She was spot-on and I got a diffuser for my office. Now kids, moms, and dads all enjoy a great-smelling office. In fact, several teen boys that completed treatment and returned for a "tune-up" session years later said they remembered the great smell in my office and said it was very calming to them. Similarly, our homes can become a calming environment for the whole family when parents maintain a positive attitude as each family member learns and grows. Our patience as parents and as a family can have a profound effect on a child whose mind is stuck in negativity.

Be Honest

Another way to use words in a respectful way is to be lovingly honest. It is too easy to say, "Great job" or "You're doing great," when in reality your child is not doing a great job. As parents, we want to support our child's efforts with lots of encouragement.

ACTIVITY

A Word Menu

Words can build, destroy, start wars, and create pictures. Words can be a gift or a dagger. King Solomon said, "A word fitly spoken is like apples of gold in a setting of silver" (Proverbs 25:11), and "He who guards his mouth and his tongue, guards his soul from troubles" (Proverbs 21:23, NASB).

Help your child learn respectful words. In a central location of your home, such as the refrigerator, post a menu of words and phrases that show respect and are helpful for your family. Be sure to model this kind of speech in your conversations with family members. Encourage your child to use the same words in his or her conversations too.

High Five

I love this exercise. In fact, I still occasionally use it with my now sixteen- and fourteen-year-old children. I used it more often when they were younger. Families I have worked with over the years have tremendously enjoyed this exercise.

The idea is to give kids a "high five" with honest words. Your child holds up a hand as if to give you a high five. You then tell:

- five things you love about him
- five things you've noticed she loves to do
- five restaurants he would love to visit
- five people who love her
- five positive things you have observed about him

But being dishonest is neither supportive nor helpful. And it can cause a lot of trust issues between you and your child when your child realizes that you've been saying "great job" to her for something she's really not very good at. Will she trust what you say when you compliment her on other things? Probably not.

One of our roles as parents is to help our children discover their unique sets of gifts and talents. Through honest encouragement and support, we guide our children to try new things, to take measured risks, and to develop the wisdom to choose some paths instead of others. If we're too uncomfortable to tell them the truth, we can prevent them from developing the discernment they need to make thoughtful and yet honest judgments about themselves.

Respect involves helping your kids understand that they can't be good at everything and helping them learn how to handle failure, disappointment, and other uncomfortable feelings. Children want to know what they are truly good at. They will either get honest feedback from you, laced with love, or the harsh reality from peers. I would rather take the opportunity to provide feedback with loving words directing my child to new and exciting opportunities than to have potentially deflating and destructive words of reality come from peers. I encourage you to practice giving honest, loving feedback about who you're discovering your child to be.

Honesty is also seen in your everyday interactions with other people. Do you exaggerate to get affirmation? Do you conveniently omit details to protect yourself? Do you stretch the truth? Are you honest about why you didn't call or text someone back? Do you admit your own faults? It feels so much better and establishes the foundation of trust when honesty is part of a home's foundation.

WHAT WE DO

In 1 Corinthians 11:1, Paul instructs his readers to imitate him as he

- five things you remember her doing when she was younger
- five things that are absolutely true about him
- five things that are unique and special about her
- five things he loves to do
- five things you wish you could do together when there is free time
- five people she loves
- five foods he loves
- five vacation spots she would love to visit
- five things you appreciate about him

Be creative and keep in mind that your child may ask for a high ten instead of a high five. I have also noticed that over time, kids start giving high fives back to their parents. I recommend doing this before bedtime or on the way to school.

imitates Christ. I love Paul's confidence, even though he also says that he is the worst of sinners. Paul recognizes his brokenness and his complete dependence on Christ. Have you noticed your kids doing things that you do—perhaps some things that are good and other things that are not so good? At the beginning of the chapter, we saw what happened when the young basketball player imitated his family. Here are some ways you can model respect in your household.

Stay Calm

Grace is the parenting trait that promotes calmness in chaos, so that parents can maintain respect. Take time to breathe and gain some perspective. Try to see the situation from the child's perspective. Be slow to speak. A helpful acronym that can be used as you gain perspective and stay calm comes from Daniel Siegel's work.[7] He created the acronym PACE. You can use PACE to move toward connection by remaining calm. PACE stands for:

- <u>Playfulness</u>—Creates flexibility of thinking, bonding, and safety. Kids love it when their parents take some time to be playful, goofy, and spontaneous. My daughter loves it when I look into her eyes with playfulness and engage with her. She sees that I'm all in with her in the moment.

- <u>Acceptance</u>—Allows "what is" and "coulds," rather than "shoulds." This does not mean accepting bad or disrespectful behavior. This means adapting to what is happening so that you can respond instead of react.

- Curiosity—The goal here is understanding rather than assuming. Your child will feel known and connected to you and will be much more open to correction and redirection.

- Empathy—This allows you to move toward an understanding of the overall experience your child is having. Your goal is to move toward compassion, kindness, and the best interest of the child.

Be On Time

How do we treat our time and other people's time? As a family, this is something we are constantly wrestling with because of our habit of being late. My wife and I both are not the most punctual people. I tend to try to squeeze as much into a minute as I can, and as a result, I frequently run at least a few minutes late. I remember someone once telling me that when I'm late it is as if my time is more important than their time. Wow! That hit me right between the eyes!

There are ripples to this. If I run late and make someone else run late, that person may be late to their next appointment or need to shorten their time with someone else. What I do truly affects others.

When I treat my spouse, kids, and others with respect, my family culture moves toward respect. I want my family to be known as respectful through our punctuality and respect of other people's time. I have learned that my wife and kids feel important when I arrive early or on time to wherever they are or wherever we need to go. I realize this can be an easy win for some, but clearly not for others. I'm still working on it.

Serve One Another

When I work with families on the topic of respect, I love the process of helping them develop a culture of cooperation in their homes. It involves service to one another and becoming contributors rather than consumers in the home, relationships, and society. This helps kids gain the understanding that life is not about fairness or only about them but about what is best for growth, development, and relationship. Kids with a contributor mindset develop resilience and are more likely to experience happiness and satisfaction in life. Who wouldn't want that?

What if kids learned early on that every person in the family plays an important role and that if someone doesn't fulfill his or her role, the entire family is affected? It's like a sports team. If someone slacks off in the game, it's much more difficult for the team to win. When framed this way, chores and household tasks become more than items on a to-do list; they are opportunities for kids to take ownership in the operation and well-being of the family and to demonstrate maturity, responsibility, and respect for the family. In this framework, kids get to be part of the "win" for the family.

Do you model service? Do you serve your spouse? Do you serve the family? Do you take time to pause your own life to help others, even when it is inconvenient? Frequently, people want our help or attention at the most inconvenient times, especially when our pace of life has no margins.

Respect Differences

People are different in many ways. As families we respect one another when we honor our different needs and ways of doing things.

Consider the adage "Good fences make good neighbors." We put up fences to outline our territory and to provide a boundary so that we don't encroach on each other's property. While the boundary places a limit between properties, it also provides freedom for property owners to use their own properties as they please.

Look at your neighbors' properties. Within the boundaries of each neighbor's property, they get to choose their plants, bushes, garden decor, home decor, house color, and more. They are free to express their likes and dislikes just as you are free to express your likes and dislikes on your property—just as long as neither party crosses the line and makes decisions about the other neighbor's property.

This idea of having freedom to pursue your own desires while respecting others' freedom to do the same also applies to families.

My son recently said he didn't like that Christmas music was being played weeks before Thanksgiving. He loves

Christmas music but felt it was too early, so he asked us if we could hold off playing Christmas music until after Thanksgiving. He didn't want to get sick of hearing Christmas songs before Christmas arrived.

However, my Christmas-loving daughter loves to sing and had just been asked to sing Christmas carols before a community play. My wife and I love Christmas too. You can imagine the dilemma this created. How could we honor the needs of the entire family?

Now, if our son asserted that he had a right to a phone or to privacy or to date, then the situation would have been very different because as parents, we have the authority to place the parameters on those areas. However, our son's request was reasonable. So our family discussed the art of compromise and collaborative problem solving, and we were able to come up with a plan together. We agreed that before Thanksgiving the rest of us would listen to Christmas music only when our son wasn't around. This compromise respected the desires of both children and gave them freedom as well as a limit.

Other limits we need to pay attention to involve how much a person can do. Some people can do a lot and never get tired, and some get overwhelmed or fatigued more easily. Get to know your own limits and your child's limits. Are they similar? Are they different? Get to know the balance that is best for your child, even if it is different from your own.

Follow Through

Over the years, I have seen well-intentioned parents overpromise and underdeliver. I myself have been known to say that we would do something, only to run out of time or money to do it. However, our actions must match the words: We need to do what we say we will do. Having integrity in this area shows respect for others at a foundational level.

Following through in the midst of a busy life is quite difficult. But to respect our families we need to honestly gauge what we will truly be able to do and then do it instead of making promises we can't keep in order to momentarily please our kids or calm them down. If we know that we can't manage something, we need to be honest about that. It's far better for our children to learn to deal with the disappointment of being told no than to have to deal with the disappointment of a parent's broken promise.

If you have overpromised and underdelivered, you have a lot of company. Most parents I know are guilty of this, especially busy and distracted parents. When kids tell me that Christians are hypocrites or that their parents are hypocrites, I tell them, "Welcome to earth." We are all guilty of hypocrisy at some point or another in our lives. That's why we need Jesus!

We should all be moving toward having more integrity in this area. While we may not reach perfection, certainly we all can grow.

Many parents make promises with the best of intentions.

They would never intend to break a promise. But we must remember that our kids trust us and believe what we tell them. They expect us to follow through. We need to speak and act with integrity. Even when they are disappointed, children feel respected when their parents are honest about what can and cannot be done. As an exercise, have your kids share times they have noticed when you overpromised or overcommitted and did not follow through. Talk about how that made them feel.

SO WHAT?

Building a foundation of respect in your relationship with your kids clearly requires a significant outlay of time, effort, and energy. The good news is that genuine respect is an investment that pays a lifetime of dividends.

Kids who understand the importance of genuine, steadfast, love-rooted respect are likely to build healthy, beneficial relationships with teachers, coaches, advisors, professors, supervisors, military superiors, law enforcement officers, and other authority figures.

Likewise, kids who have been shown respect from an early age are likely to develop a strong sense of personal value and worth. They are less likely to be swayed by peer pressure or the opinions of others. They are less likely to struggle with self-image issues. They are better equipped to handle setbacks.

Such is the power of respect.

Ripples

Have you ever tossed a rock into a pond and watched the ripples move across the water? What we do affects others like ripples across a pond. Those ripples grow and spread outward long after the rock was first tossed into the water.

We ripple into each other's lives all day long in helpful and not-so-helpful ways. When we encourage one another, it can ripple into encouragement from that person to another and so on. If we make fun of someone, that person may make fun of someone else and the ripple continues on and on.

I can still remember the wonderful ripples from my grandparents. My grandpa taught me to garden, and to this day I love gardening. He talked to me about God and displayed respect and love for everyone, including strangers. His ripples continue in my life. I can also remember when a girl I thought was cute at camp in fifth grade called me a fat geek. Even though that is not my identity, I felt those ripples for a while.

I can remember when a six-foot-nine, insecure freshman boy was depantsed in front of some students (including girls) watching our basketball practice. He was humiliated. So he went on to put out a broken chair for an overweight girl to sit on, and she flattened it in front of the whole class. She was humiliated as well and left the classroom crying. She stayed in the bathroom the entire class period, sobbing.

Ripples.

Remember that what we say and do can continue living in someone else.

Help your children recognize the ripples they have received today, during the past week, and throughout their lives so far. Who have been the contributors and consumers, the encouragers and discouragers, the influencers and distractors in their lives? How have people rippled into their lives? How have they rippled into other people's lives? How far do our words and actions go in other people's lives?

RESPECT

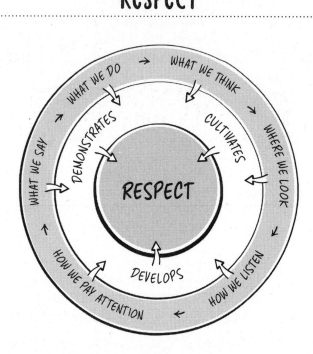

WHAT WE DO → WHAT WE THINK →

WHAT WE SAY ↗ DEMONSTRATES CULTIVATES WHERE WE LOOK

RESPECT

HOW WE PAY ATTENTION DEVELOPS HOW WE LISTEN

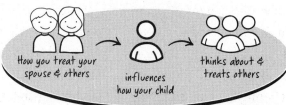

How you treat your spouse & others → influences how your child → thinks about & treats others

ACTIONS

- Remember important events
- Be present mentally, emotionally & physically
- Renew your mind through prayer & God's Word
- Model respect by seeing others through God's eyes
- Imitate Christ

CHAPTER 4

INTENTIONALITY

When you get right down to it,
intentional living is about living your best story.
–JOHN MAXWELL

The heart of man plans his way,
but the LORD establishes his steps.
–PROVERBS 16:9

TIME CAN FLY LIKE A SUPERSONIC JET. I did not fully believe this until I became a parent. I remember thinking to myself when my son was three and my daughter was one that adulthood was a long way away for both of them. But suddenly, my son is taller than me and has a lower voice than me. My daughter is a young woman, and she and I are talking about what to look for in a man as she considers dating in the next few years. Where did the time go?

I have met with countless parents who have said they wish they'd done this or that differently. Some say that if they could do it all over again, they would reprioritize what they did as parents. They would spend more time with their kids, especially during the younger years when children were at home and didn't have jobs, places to go, cars to drive, or friends to see. The reality is that we do the best we can with what we've got. We simply don't have the time or energy to adjust to everything life throws at us, and schedules seem to get busier at each age and stage of a child's development. We feel regret when we look back and evaluate ourselves and the jobs we've done as parents.

We all feel this way as we look back in hindsight. But there is something we can do to minimize this feeling of our realities being out of sync with our desires for our family lives.

Intentionality can help us feel that we have more control over the direction of our parenting. Intentionality is simply a matter of knowing what you want to do to make each day count in your child's life and in your opportunity to be transformed as you embrace the challenge and responsibility of being a parent. It is not about indulging your child and making your home an activity- or child-focused home.

A few years ago, I had the privilege of working with a couple who were seeking help with their thirteen-year-old son, the youngest of three boys. Unlike his parents and two older brothers, this young man—Ryan—was having difficulty coping with everyday life. He was struggling with chronic anxiety, nervousness, and insomnia, so something needed to be done. The more we talked, the clearer it became that he was in need of serious help.

When I asked for his side of the story, Ryan was ready with an answer. "The problem," he said, "is that I'm totally stressed out. My family is too busy! We're always going somewhere, doing something, adding another commitment to the calendar. I never get any downtime! It's too much, and I wish we could hang out more as a family!"

The interesting thing was that nobody else in the family seemed to share his feelings. In fact, they seemed to like their hectic schedule and they didn't have an intentional plan for connecting with each other. Rather, they valued sports and school. Ryan's mom and dad weren't bad parents. They were just highly motivated people who maintained an active involvement in everything from work to church to the local community to their sons' educational and extracurricular activities. Ryan's brothers seemed perfectly satisfied with the fast pace of their family's busy lifestyle but were struggling in their life choices. The rest of the family had a hard time understanding why Ryan didn't see things the way they did.

The family's pace of life didn't allow time for reflection and connection with each other and God. Ryan's parents were used to pursuing, but intentionality means knowing when to slow things down or just simply stop.

My suggestion for this family was to intentionally balance rest, relationship, and work in their lives, and to be aware that different members of the family have different needs. This may seem obvious, but finding such balance is hard, especially when we add technology, entertainment, and the endless menu of possible distractions and pursuits to the mix. Intentional parenting begins with pausing to determine what you're pursuing and why you're pursuing it.

Many people have been led to believe that an intentional parent is a perfect parent, which is not true. There are many things I have started with a great deal of intention that I didn't completely follow through on, including a weekly family meeting in our home. But we try our best to have intentional conversations and time together. I have yet to meet a family that has been perfectly intentional along the way. However, I can tell you about many couples who are thankful they have learned to be more intentional in their parenting because of what it did for them, their kids, and their family.

THE RELATIONAL PARENT

Intentional parents pay attention to the relationships between family members. They parent through relationships with their children. Family specialist Carol Watson-Phillips has gone to great lengths to describe relational parenting in a study entitled "Relational Fathering: Sons Liberate Dads."[1] Watson-Phillips defines a "relational father" as one who:

- builds connection
- repairs relationships
- has self-awareness
- tackles challenges
- listens and pays attention
- works hard at communicating
- is intentional about rearranging his schedule
- makes himself available

- sees fathering as a relationship and an honor and not a job or simply a role
- prioritizes and pursues what is important rather than what is urgent
- has grace
- carefully considers the power of his words, both good and bad
- recognizes the endless opportunities for personal growth
- is willing to define masculinity in terms of relationship and caring

As Watson-Phillips points out, this model of fatherhood is countercultural. It's also completely compatible with our Christian faith, which portrays God as a loving Heavenly Father.[2] Scripture tells us that God our Father:

- knows us intimately
- loves us deeply
- always has our best in mind
- provides for our needs
- lovingly corrects us
- is always approachable through prayer
- gives us good gifts
- invites us to call Him Abba (Daddy)

The picture of relational parenting presented by Carol Watson-Phillips is that of a parent who understands the need to keep striving to make things right. That, of course, takes energy, focus, discipline, and attention. And that's what intentionality is really all about.

INTENTIONALITY AND SPONTANEITY

Effective intentionality doesn't mean that you approach parenting like a computer or an automaton. On the contrary, intentionality combines order and deliberation with freedom, creativity, and spontaneity. This means intentionally pressing pause in your own life to let your life intersect with your child's. Laughter and play are perfect examples of essential, spontaneous, pause-button moments. My kids love it when I take time to be playful or goofy with them. To be honest, I don't always have the energy for this, but I know it can create connection in the moment. My kids also like it when I spontaneously ask them to go for a walk or go out to breakfast, lunch, or dinner. Spontaneity is about not being too busy to enjoy relationships and taking the time to intentionally enter unplanned moments.

Unplanned moments can include teachable moments. I can guarantee you that I've missed many teachable moments in my children's lives. But that doesn't make me weak in intentionality. It simply reflects the sheer number of teachable opportunities that arise. Daily life, sports, nature, and entertainment are just a few of the areas that offer opportunities for spontaneous teaching moments. Here are some ideas for taking advantage of teachable moments:

Daily life: Reflect on what is and isn't going well in daily life. Talk about the challenges of living in an imperfect—and sometimes unfair—world. Emphasize that our ultimate success or failure often boils down to whom we listen to. Are we listening closely to God as we engage in the incredible journeys and adventures of life?

Sports: Perhaps your daughter persevered when she wanted to quit. Perhaps your son's team pulled off an upset through teamwork. Perhaps your child is taking a loss very hard. Perhaps your daughter has been coached by someone with a win-at-all-costs mentality. There's no shortage of teachable moments in the sports world.

Nature: If your children help you with a garden, you can talk about the importance of having good soil, providing the right nutrients, and bearing fruit—in the garden and in life. You can marvel over the beauty and intricate design of God's universe. You can explore questions such as, "Why

Goal-Setting Retreat

Consider holding an annual goal-setting time with your own family. Dr. Richard Lytle recently spoke to the management staff at Focus on the Family on leadership. He is the father of three grown daughters, as well as a husband, professor, speaker, and board member at Focus on the Family. In his presentation, he shared about the annual goal-setting retreats he and his wife led for their family while their three daughters were growing up in their home. They would plan a fun fall retreat during which family members set physical, spiritual, mental, and relational goals for the coming year. They would seek God's guidance and share their goals with one another. They would also encourage each other throughout the year.

are humans the only beings who are given the ability to reason and choose?"

Entertainment: Sometimes I'll pause a movie that we're watching as a family to ask my kids what they think it would be like to be different characters in the film. Call it a quick lesson in empathy. Your family's entertainment choices also offer opportunities to consider and discuss the importance of not getting distracted in our relationships with God.

INTENTIONALITY AND PERSONALITY DIFFERENCES

Ryan's story demonstrates how appreciating personality differences can affect the way you apply intentional parenting techniques in your home. Before you can devise a workable strategy for relating effectively to each child, you have to understand what makes each child tick. You also need to have a good grasp of your own temperament and how it interacts with your children's temperaments. For example, if you're an extrovert and your son or daughter is an introvert, you're going to have to be aware of the distinctions between you and take them into account. There's no such thing as a one-size-fits-all plan for successful parenting. Intentional parenting is relational parenting, and relationship is an art, not a science.

I once met a very intentional mom and dad. The couple had four children, a clean home, and a consistent routine that involved all of their kids. Their kids naturally had different personalities and interests. The parents took their individual traits into account as they developed their family routines.

One child tended to be quite opinionated, so they provided him some leadership roles in their system and often asked for his opinion on ways to improve the overall system. Another child tended to be creative, so she helped with designing visuals and brainstorming ideas for the family's cleaning system. Another son was more social, so he was given roles that involved communication and helped facilitate family meetings to make sure the family remained a team in conquering the house. The fourth child was a bit more sincere than the others and was put in charge of making sure everyone did what they said they were going to do.

These parents found ways to utilize the strengths of each child's personality in their family's routines. While the family may sound perfect, the parents would be the first to admit that they all needed to constantly reset, repair, and regroup because of the imperfections that spilled out due to the many differences in the home. However, if we don't intentionally guide personality differences, these differences may create chaos, conflict, and exhaustion in the home. This couple used their strength in intentionality to more effectively manage their kids' differences.

My point here is that each child is unique. Some are inattentive to detail, while others are overly attentive. Some take risks while others prefer the safety of a stable routine. Some are anxious. Some are uninhibited and blissfully unaware of the impact of their words and actions on other people. Still others have physical, mental, or emotional problems that require the expert attention of a specialist.

Parents and Sports

I enjoy coaching my son's basketball team. But the experience has made me painfully aware of the bad things that can happen when moms and dads are distracted from their real goals by the desire to see their kids succeed on the court. That's why I've made it a standard practice to get all of my players' families together at the beginning of the season for what I consider the most important pep talk of the year. When everybody's relaxed and having a good time, I stand up and make the following appeal.

"Look around the room," I say, glancing at my intergenerational audience. "The fact of the matter is that only a very small percentage of these boys will end up participating in sports at the college or professional level. Meanwhile, all of them are going to grow up to be men. All of them need your time, understanding, affection, guidance, encouragement, and personal attention. Each one desperately wants to know that he is known and loved just as he is."

I have two reasons for emphasizing these points. In the first place, I've noticed that some parents get sidetracked by the intensity of the game. They start to value success in sports above all else. *My son needs to be the best on the team*, they think, *or else!* This mindset fosters a critical attitude that can wreak havoc on the parent-child relationship.

In the second place, I've seen how an inordinate emphasis on sports can lead to a schedule that exhausts the whole family and leaves everyone with little or no time for building healthy connections in the home. Mothers and fathers need to remember that it's those connections, and not a shelf full of trophies, that will one day be the measure of their success as parents. Your children's time in sports, music, theater, band, choir, and any other activity is about them learning to develop the talents they've been given. Your role is to guide, correct, encourage, and enjoy their growth as you learn what they do well and what they enjoy doing.

Please don't misunderstand me. This is not about making your children feel good; it's about helping them grow toward who God created them to be. Our kids need to learn that their identities are in who they are in Christ and not in what they accomplish. What they do will naturally flow from who they are in Christ.

The intentional parent is the mom or dad who is comfortable with his or her own personality strengths and challenges. The intentional parent is one who willingly invests the time and energy necessary to learn about each child's unique personality and teaches him or her how to most effectively use that personality to accomplish goals and relate well to others.

Out of that deeply personal and relational understanding comes the ability for the parent to mentor, correct, and teach each child utilizing the other six traits of effective parenting—love, respect, boundaries, grace, gratitude, and adaptability.

INTENTIONALITY: INGREDIENTS FOR PARENTAL GROWTH

It's one thing to understand the theory behind intentionality in parenting. It's something else to develop the skills required to put that theory into practice.

Take a garden, for example. After you intentionally plan, prepare the soil, and sow seeds, you must pay attention to the plant by fertilizing and watering it to help it thrive. These same steps are necessary as you take on intentionality as a parent.

Plan

Being an intentional parent means taking time to figure out where you're going and why you're going that way. It's about having a direction and pointing your family in that direction. This can include making plans for your kids' spiritual growth, as well as making plans for events such as camps, activities, family time, and holidays. Though planning may not come easily to everyone, it's essential for using time well and being prepared for various stages and activities as they come.

Planning involves developing and communicating values and character traits you want to make sure your kids learn along the way. What character traits do you want your kids to learn? Answering that question in the planning stage of parenting will help you focus on the best teachable moments as they occur spontaneously in daily life.

Planning mealtimes together is a great place to focus your attention. A study published in *The American Journal of Family Therapy* found that consistent family mealtimes result in increased family satisfaction and communication.[3] You can make mealtimes fun by incorporating games, questions, and other activities that encourage interaction. When things are going really well, celebrate by having a mealtime watching a movie together and enjoying one another's company. Be creative and introduce some variety to your mealtime plans.

As you make plans, keep in mind that intentionality involves time, one of our most precious possessions. Decide exactly how you're going to invest yourself in your children's lives.

Intentional planning includes the development of traditions in the home. Do you have a "bedtime ritual" that you go through with your kids? It might go something like this: brush teeth, get into bed, read a story, say prayers, and then get one last drink of water before turning out the lights. If you do something like this regularly, you've established a tradition. Traditions can extend into every area of family life. They can

ACTIVITY

Investment-Chart Exercise

How you spend your time shows what you're committed to—what you're invested in. As a family, make investment charts to help children understand that they need to make intentional choices about how they spend their time. Discuss how each family member is investing his or her time. Place a numeric value on each investment according to its importance, with the total of investments being 100. (For young children, you could use a simple numbered ranking system.) For example, a child might say that spending time with friends playing video games is his number one investment, so connection with friends is very valuable to him. He may give it a value of 30, followed by sports at 25, family at 20,

include things like going out to dinner every Sunday night, making pancakes or waffles on Saturday mornings, sharing things for which you're grateful around the table at Thanksgiving, watching favorite holiday movies, or talking about God's gift in Jesus Christ at Christmas. It doesn't matter what specific traditions you choose to implement. What counts is that you use these traditions to create bonds between the generations and establish a corporate identity for your home. Again, this is something that doesn't happen automatically, at least not in our hectic world. It has to be developed intentionally.

Pay Attention

We discussed paying attention to your child in chapter 3, but it applies to intentionality just as much as it does to respect. You can see that parents who pay attention are showing respect *and* intentionality *and* steadfast love toward their children. As you work through the seven traits of effective parenting, you'll notice that a number of the strategies fit into more than one category.

Attention is a critical ingredient in helping a child thrive in Christ. If you don't know your child well, you can't intentionally respond to him or her as a parent. We live in an era of texts, quick video clips, and sound bites. Shortened and undisciplined attention spans are written off as the by-products of our screen-centric lives—an unfortunate but seemingly unavoidable reality in our new cultural landscape. Don't believe it. The ability to control your attention is a skill that can be retained (or reacquired, as the case may be) and sharpened with time, practice, and instruction. I'll go a step further and say that it's a skill you *must* develop if you want to be an intentional and relational parent.

Throughout Scripture, God's people are told to pay attention. We need constant reminders to stay focused as we navigate the many things vying for our attention. I wish I could say this is easy, but it is quite difficult. Controlling your attention

and so on. This opens up a great discussion about the intentional decisions we each must make according to our values, time, and energy.

Compare the investments chart to what God tells us to invest ourselves in—prayer, Scripture, people, and serving God and His Kingdom. Add any other things you have noticed in your time reading Scripture that God wants us to invest in (e.g., orphans and widows). Discuss with your family the need to be balanced and healthy in how you spend your time.

The Spotlight

What is it that most easily captures and holds your attention? Here's a little activity that can help you and your kids think about what it means to stay focused on the right things.

In a theater, the audience's attention is guided and fixed by the movements of the spotlight. Create your own home theater by gathering the whole family in the living room. Bring along a flashlight and turn out all the other lights. Have some fun passing the flashlight around and giving each person a chance to place the spotlight wherever he or she chooses. You can point the beam wherever you like—at a chair across the room, the television screen, a painting on the wall, or another person's face.

requires much energy and diligence. It involves making choices and being aware of when your focus has wandered. It involves understanding what pulls your attention away and why. Where your attention goes, you go. More to the point: What you pay attention to determines how well you connect with your kids.

Part of paying attention is being a noticer. Train yourself and your kids to be noticers of how God is working in your home, your lives, and your community. Be a noticer of others. How are they uniquely designed by God? What are they doing well? Notice when people make great decisions and celebrate with them. Notice when people need God's love or an encouraging word. Part of being a noticer is being a genuine listener. Being attentive and providing honest and loving feedback provides the authenticity kids love. Give them a true mirror of who they are by giving them honest words about their value as children of Christ. It is important to learn discernment so that you can distinguish between what to be concerned about and what to let go.

Attention also plays a key role in whether you subscribe to pessimistic or optimistic thinking. The pessimist focuses on the negative and the optimist focuses on the positive; however, the circumstances are exactly the same. The distinction lies entirely in the mindsets of the two individuals. Similarly, the critic is wired to obsess on mistakes and errors, while the encourager tends to see flaws as gifts and recognizes the potential that lies beneath the surface. This is exactly what Paul was getting at in Philippians 4:8: "Whatever is true, whatever is honorable, whatever is just, whatever is pure, whatever is lovely, whatever is commendable, if there is any excellence, if there is anything worthy of praise, think about these things." Paul learned what to pay attention to as he followed Christ.

In Isaiah 26:3 we read, "You keep him in perfect peace whose mind is stayed on you, because he trusts in you." A steadily attentive mind is

Tell your kids, "Wherever you shine the light, that's what you're going to see." Underscore the idea that this is a conscious choice. Then ask some questions like, "Where do you fix your spotlight? On celebrity, fame, wealth, and power—or on the needs of others?" Talk about what it means to direct our attention toward building relationships with other members of the family.

essential to inward peace. Many of us lack peace because it can be quite difficult for us to say no. After all, there are many good things to say yes to. As a result, we are completely at the mercy of the barrage of opportunities that come our way every day. It becomes difficult for us to see that intentionality is about paying attention to the things that matter most—namely, human relationships.

Where does God direct His attention when He turns His eyes toward His children? Isaiah 66:2 says, "But this is the one to whom I will look: he who is humble and contrite in spirit and trembles at my word." In other words, God is looking for someone who is capable of setting his or her attention: a person who is willing to keep turning and shaping his or her inward attention until it outwardly aligns with the values and priorities of the Lord. And since God's priorities are wrapped up in relationships, it stands to reason that the more intentional we are about connecting with Him, the more intentional we will become about connecting with our children and other people.

Follow Through

Another ingredient in the intentional parenting formula is authentically caring by following through. This can also be described as faithfulness or consistency.

This is another topic that we covered in chapter 3. Let's discuss how following through applies to intentionality.

In this case, I'm speaking in particular about the importance of doing what we say we're going to do, which sounds like a no-brainer but actually can be very difficult! When we're worn out from working too hard or moving too fast, we can easily apply our efforts to what's urgent rather than what's important. When we're exhausted, we often try to appease our children by promising to give them what they want "later." If that's your modus operandi, make sure that you don't forget to keep your promises.

Our choices and our actions show our kids what we value. This is especially crucial when urgent things are knocking loudly at our doors. When we focus on the noisy, urgent things, it can be all too easy to neglect the quiet, less demanding things that are of rock-solid importance to us. Make choices based on the people and values that are important to you, not on urgency.

I recently got to practice this discipline. I was working on tight deadlines, writing a paper for my doctoral program and writing an article for the Focus on the Family website, when my daughter came to me. "Dad, do you have time?" What a powerful question! And what a dilemma!

On the one hand, I felt the pull of my personal and professional responsibilities. On the other hand, my parental instincts were telling me, *You have to drop what you're doing and connect with Lexi. She needs to talk.*

I pressed pause in my mind. I smiled at my daughter and said, "Yes, I have time, but I need to get back to these responsibilities. Let me finish this paragraph, and then we'll talk." She understood the boundary but felt listened to. She also felt valued when I emerged from my office a few minutes later and showed her that I meant what I'd said. I was willing to set aside what I was doing in order to pay attention to her. In that moment,

I had to differentiate between what was urgent and what was important—something that's not always easy to do. There have been plenty of moments when I've gotten sucked into the urgent and let the important fly by. This was one time I did it right.

The bottom line is that as parents, we are not trying to win a trophy. Instead, our task is to develop strong bonds with our kids. When we authentically care by keeping our word and intentionally following through on our promises, we show our children how much we value those connections. When we fail, we can confess our faults, busyness, and distractibility, and ask for forgiveness. Either way, we have an opportunity to deepen the whole family's understanding of mercy, grace, and balancing the urgent and the important.

Get Involved

Another way to express intentionality is to get inside your children's world and become a part of their activities and interests. Be a connector. Connect to your children. Connect family members to one another. Find or develop common interests with your children. Learn to enjoy what they enjoy. If your daughter participates in sports, try to attend as many games (or practices) as you can. If your son plays in the school orchestra, make his concerts and recitals events of top priority in the pages of your monthly planner. You cannot get a second chance to attend an event—once the moment has passed, it's in the past. Whether they admit it or not, kids feel loved when parents show an interest in the things that interest them. Most kids desire time over things and experiences over gifts.

Take time to laugh, play, and know your child. Write things down to remember. We all love to be noticed and authentically known. Help connect your kids to God, their heavenly Father and Savior. There are endless connection points throughout each day.

Get involved in your children's lives by being a builder with your words. God can use your words in magnificent ways. Ephesians 4:29 says, "Let no corrupting talk come out of your mouths, but only such as is good for building up, as fits the occasion, that it may give grace to those who hear." The words that you speak into your children's lives can build them up in amazing ways. You can mold their characters. You can guide them away from harmful things and toward good things. You can encourage them to make wise choices. But to choose the best words and the best moment to say them, you must know what's going on in your children's lives and hearts by being involved in their everyday lives. Model being a builder of others through loving, constructive, honest, and encouraging words.

Intentional involvement also includes learning your child's personal "love language" and figuring out how to use it on a daily basis. In his very popular Five Love Languages books, Dr. Gary Chapman teaches that people receive and communicate love in one of five primary ways: words of affirmation, quality time, receiving gifts, acts of service, and physical touch. Being intentional means investing the time and effort to express your love for your kids in terms that they can understand.

For example, my daughter, Lexi, loves physical touch, especially drawing together in close proximity. My son, Alex, wants me to spend lots of quality time with him, whether that means shooting hoops together, building things with wood, or just going for a walk. My role as a dad is to manage my day in such a way that I have opportunities to pause in my busyness to connect in loving ways with my kids so that I influence their lives. Remember, they truly become who they listen to and they listen to those to whom they are close.

Set Boundaries

Kids also crave consistent boundaries. Be intentional about setting limits with technology. Intentionality in this area can help reduce entertainment-related disasters in your home, including the dark reality of pornography. Putting filters on computers and devices is a great start. Initiating frequent conversations about entertainment choices and temptations is even better.

Focus on the Family designed the Plugged In website for the very purpose of intentionally creating technology and entertainment intelligence. At PluggedIn.com you can read reviews with your kids about video games, music, books, television, and movies. Your kids face decisions every day. The choices they make will depend on their influences. The question is, will they be influenced by social media, technology, peers, teachers, news outlets—or by you?

KNOWING THE DIFFERENCE

Are you familiar with Reinhold Niebuhr's famous "Serenity Prayer"? The first four lines go like this:

God, grant me the serenity
to accept the things I
cannot change,
the courage to change the
things I can,
and the wisdom to know
the difference.[4]

Intentionality in parenting is all about knowing that difference. The longer you live and the more experience you have raising children, the more deeply you will understand that there are plenty of things in this world—things about yourself, your kids, and the circumstances in which you live—that can't be controlled.

Intentionality is a matter of identifying those things that can be controlled and then doing something about them. It's about choosing the values you want to emphasize in your home and taking deliberate steps—baby steps, if necessary—toward making them the foundation of your family's experience together.

Personalizing Philippians 4:8
Looking for a way to heighten your family's awareness of and attention to the good things about one another? Try this simple activity. Get everyone together around the table or in the living room and read Philippians 4:8. Then assign each person the name of another family member. After that, take turns rereading the verse and inserting that family member's name into the text: "Finally, brothers, whatever is true about Dad (or Mom or David or Jenny), whatever is honorable, whatever is just, whatever is pure . . . think about such things." It's a great way to redirect the perceptions and attitudes that shape interpersonal relationships within your home.

KEY TAKEAWAYS
CHAPTER 4
INTENTIONALITY

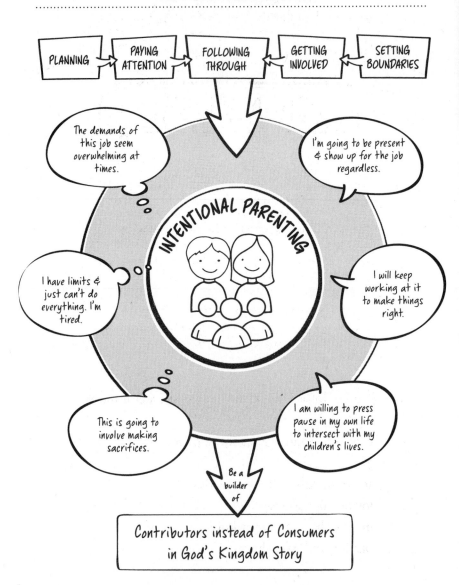

STEADFAST LOVE

*For I am sure that neither death nor life, nor angels
nor rulers, nor things present nor things to come,
nor powers, nor height nor depth, nor anything
else in all creation, will be able to separate us from
the love of God in Christ Jesus our Lord.*

−ROMANS 8:38-39

*To be loved by God is the highest relationship,
the highest achievement, and the highest position in life.*

−HENRY BLACKABY

WHAT DOES IT MEAN TO BE a loving parent? Does it mean:

- providing food, water, and shelter?
- giving hugs?
- spending time with your kids?
- loving your spouse?
- buying things for your kids?
- playing with your kids?

- listening to your kids?
- going on trips as a family?
- laughing together?
- telling your kids that you love them?

In reality, it can mean all of those things and so much more. The Focus on the Family Research and Insight Lab recently surveyed parents about what it means to be a loving parent. There were dozens of responses! In truth, *everything* that good parents do for their children is motivated by a deep, steadfast, sacrificial love that is like no other love.

Love as a parent may appear simple on the surface, but it's much more complex than one could imagine. There are few relationships that have as much potential for pain, sacrifice, and love as the parent-child relationship.

I recently observed my son and daughter and contemplated God's incredible work in creating them. I thanked Him for giving me the opportunity to be their dad and to have a part in molding them as human beings. I paused to notice how they are unique and yet have some similarities to their mom and me. I contemplated the design of their thoughts, emotions, beliefs, perceptions, experiences, pursuits, and interests. I was struck by how incredible and humbling it is that we get to contribute to, influence, and encourage our kids as they are molded, shaped, and set free to serve God's Kingdom. My eyes welled up, and I was amazed and grateful. *I have a son! I have a daughter!* I thought. *I'm a rich man!*

Love is truly the glue that connects us in an imperfect

world—and it begins with parental love: God's love for us, our love for our kids. The worse the brokenness we see in the world, the more glue is needed.

Using the state-and-city illustration, love is:

- the building material for a steadfast foundation for the structures of the cities
- the fuel to build healthy and thriving cities and states
- the material for building, maintaining, and repairing roads and bridges between cities
- the spotlights that illuminate the monuments of the cities
- the artwork and other treasures archived in the cities' museums
- brought to the cities in endless supply by contributors, influencers, encouragers, and the Master Architect

As parents we have the opportunity to see and experience the depths of love in action. This is the kind of love that can change the world. But it begins in us. True, steadfast parental love changes our perspective and changes us emotionally, mentally, and spiritually.

A FOUNDATION OF LOVE

Steadfast love is absolutely foundational to parenting. Parenting begins with love, and that love figures prominently in the other six traits of effective parenting.

ADAPTABILITY

Love provides the insight and perspective to be adaptable. It brings the necessary ingredients of patience, empathy, and wisdom to provide what is necessary and unique to each child as he or she is guided toward understanding his or her identity in Christ. Adaptability allows for collaboration between family members. Love means we are pliable and able to be created into a new being like clay in a potter's hand.

RESPECT

Love drives us toward a respectful attitude as we faithfully and wholeheartedly step into our roles as parent and spouse. It helps us see the incredible value of the relationships we have in front of us. Steadfast love shapes the lenses through which we see our children as we learn about them and help them pursue what God wants for their lives. Do we see our children as God's? This perspective will motivate us to show respect as we interact with them.

INTENTIONALITY

Intentional parenting infused with love is genuine and connecting. Intentionality pursues spiritual growth and closeness. Parents can model intentional love by prioritizing personal relationships with God and others and facilitating ongoing conversations with God and others in their day-to-day lives.

Wired for Love

Let's talk about the changes our brains experience when we become parents. God has wired us to experience those changes. A mom's brain begins to change at her baby's conception. Oxytocin is released, which is the bonding hormone our bodies secrete as we attach emotionally with one another.

The mom's brain changes to respond more effectively and attentively to the newborn's needs. The main changes in the brain are centered on memory and attention. A mom's brain may become more attentive and attuned to her child's cries and facial expressions. Her brain may also become more efficient and specialized in tasks associated with caring for an infant/child.

God has essentially wired a mom to develop the psychological tools that make her an attentive, attuned, and effective mom. The challenge is learning how to use the tools well while dealing with old habits, current emotions, exhaustion, stress, and perceptions.

A dad's brain also changes, beginning at the birth of his child, depending on the amount of time he spends with his newborn. Dad's brain can have similar changes to Mom's brain. A dad's brain releases oxytocin, the bonding hormone, as he spends time with his kids. In addition, his brain can have cell growth in the regions associated with attention, memory, and navigation.

A dad's brain can also decrease the body's level of testosterone the more time he spends with his child and family. A testosterone decrease can make a man more cooperative and sensitive. In fact, some friends of mine have asked me why they were crying more often when watching movies. These guys tend to spend as much time as possible with their kids, family, and spouse. They and their family are benefiting from the changes God had designed to happen.

BOUNDARIES

Boundaries are necessary for relationships. Love recognizes and teaches the purpose for boundaries. Steadfast love provides the building blocks toward trusted and meaningful boundaries through the provision of safety, trust, and relationship.

GRACE AND FORGIVENESS

Steadfast love provides a reason for grace and forgiveness to exist. God is love, and He gives us countless opportunities for "do-overs." Love provides the flexibility in a relationship to have "do-overs" for connection and reconnection.

GRATITUDE

A loving parent is a grateful parent. Gratitude is loving what you have rather than demanding what you want. Gratitude invites the humility needed to have full dependence on God as we parent our children. My steadfast love for my kids fuels my gratitude for the time I get to be with them. I'm thankful to be a dad. It is changing me and taking me to depths of love that I would've never reached had I never had children.

THE FIRST TIME

My children wouldn't remember, but I sure do. I remember the first time I held each of them. I didn't care that I was hungry and tired. Holding my children for the first time was like no other experience before or after. It was as if a switch was flipped, and a bond like no other began to grow.

I envision the love I had experienced up to the point of being a dad as soil being prepared for a seed to grow. The soil had been nourished and the seeds were able to take root because of the way my parents had loved me. My parents' love for me was sacrificial. My dad took on three jobs when I was around nine years old so that we could live in the United States. My mom worked long hours as a teacher. They both faithfully took us to church. It would have been much more comfortable for my dad to continue in an executive position in Mexico, but my mom and dad decided the sacrifice for our spiritual well-being was worth the cost as we moved to Colorado Springs. My parents had many moments of imperfection, as we all do, but they provided a foundation of steadfast love for our home.

I remember feeling an overwhelming love for my kids as I held them and cared for them. The foundations of love that I had experienced laid the groundwork for my love for my kids.

I understand that not everyone has received sacrificial love growing up; some have soil that is dry and lacks the nutrients needed for growing seeds. In these cases, love is not automatic and may be unbalanced. It is important to understand the impact this can have on people's abilities to naturally love and grow in their love for their children. The truth is that all of us are broken in one way or another. None of us has been loved perfectly, and none of us loves perfectly. And yet, God is gracious. And through His restoration and love, we all can learn to love others in healthy ways.

FOUR STAGES OF LOVE

There are four stages people go through in life as they mature toward the ultimate form of deep-rooted and "ninja-level" steadfast love in parenting.[1]

I Love Me for Me

This begins when we're born. We love out of survival. We cry, yell, scream, and hit in order to get what we need. We are truly pursuing our own needs at this stage.

Unfortunately, some adults get stuck here and don't really mature. They most likely never received the love they needed to move on to the next stage. They love out of their own needs and not out of wanting to love others or caring about the well-being of others. Their love is out of survival. These are individuals who either leave their families or are involved in severe addictions, abuse, or domestic violence. They tend to be reactive and disconnected as adults. They are concerned only about being in their own cities and are not concerned or interested in connection. They are only interested in escaping, controlling, or being alone.

I Love You for Me

Toddlers begin to show this as they learn who brings them comfort, connection, safety, love, and enjoyment. They love the people who take care of them.

Some adults get stuck in this stage and continue to love others for their own needs and benefit. This may be shown in parents who yell at their children to perform better. The parent, in this case, feels a sense of fear that he or she will look bad if his or her child fails or performs poorly. Another way this plays out is through guilt trips. The parent might say to the child, "You don't spend enough time with me, so I feel sad and depressed." The child is held responsible for her parent's emotions, which is similar to a toddler blaming others for her emotions. To an extreme, narcissists tend to love others as a benefit to themselves. They blame others if there are issues or disappointments. This level is like a city constantly consuming and receiving without visiting or even noticing other cities, much less developing two-way connections with them.

I Love You for You

We may first learn this during our preschool years as we interact with others cooperatively and with self-control. This is a sacrificial love—a love that seeks the best for the other. As adults, this can be a respectful, altruistic type of love. I can say that many moms would land in this category.

I can still remember a few occasions where my mom told us, "No one appreciates the work I do. Everyone can just make their own food. I am going to sleep and rest all day." She was clearly sad, a bit depressed, and upset. It would usually come out of nowhere. She was a teacher, volunteer at church, friend, wife, and mom and became exhausted without any of us knowing or realizing that she was reaching that point.

There are some moms and dads who are completely drained and feel they have given everything and end up disconnecting out of resentment or exhaustion. They serve and give until they shrivel up like a raisin if there is no self-care.

This third level is like a city constantly noticing, building, or connecting with other cities and, in the process, severely neglecting its own needs.

I Love Me for You

This stage involves loving yourself well, much as Jesus did during His ministry. It involves recharging in order to love fully, attentively, and wisely. It means doing the necessary things to take care of yourself like praying, spending time in Scripture, resting, eating well, exercising, and enjoying fellowship with others. With this kind of love, the individual takes care of him or herself to become a gift to others. And the better we take care of ourselves, the better we'll be at being engaged and responsive to our children.

This fourth level is like a city that prepares for visitors. The city genuinely cares about the visitors' experiences and wants to notice, build, and connect with other cities. The city loves its own city and wants others to be a part of the continued building and thriving of the city. At the same time, they want surrounding cities to thrive as well.

You have the privilege of truly influencing, contributing to, and encouraging your children along the way as they discover who God has created them to be. It is important not to try to create a carbon copy of yourself. There is only room for one you in this universe. Your child needs to be who God has created him or her to be.

PROVISION

Families are made up of imperfect people trying to do life together day in and day out. This leaves plenty of opportunity for love to shine. I believe that steadfast love in parenting is all about provision. There are five essentials that loving parents provide for their children: basic needs, relationship, boundaries, direction, and identity.

There is an interesting relationship between these five essentials that is illustrated in the pyramid diagram below. The first two essentials, basic needs and relationship, develop a

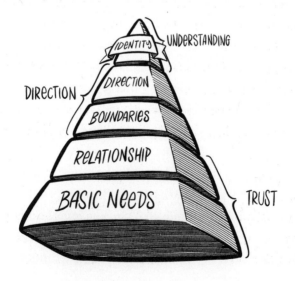

foundation of trust in our kids. This foundation gives children security as they move on toward boundaries, direction, and then identity. Let's explore these five essentials in more detail.

1. Basic Needs

Loving parents provide for the basic needs of their children. Infants need food, burping, sleep, diaper changes, warmth, safety, and security. As parents provide these consistently in response to the infant's need, the parents build the foundation of trust in the relationship. Of course, it takes a bit for parents to get the hang of interpreting their infant's cries. But over time, parents and infants learn to understand one another and find a rhythm of care that works for them. The infant learns that the parent can be counted on to provide for him or her. This creates an initial bond between infant and parent.

This kind of trust building can also happen with older children at the beginning of a blended family as the children learn that the new stepparent can be counted on to provide for their needs.

I love to see parents provide this first level of love. Many kids don't even have their basic needs met, which breaks my heart.

2. Relationship

Meeting your children's basic needs provides the necessary foundation to build relationship. Loving parents build relationship with their children. In our neighborhood, there is a dad I sometimes see outside with his kids. I love to glance and see how he interacts with his two daughters and one son. I have seen him playing basketball with his kids, making up wiffle ball baseball games for the entire family to play in their front yard, wrestling and playing football with his young son, and taking the time to coach and guide his kids in the sports they choose. He sometimes has to travel for work, but when he is home, he is all in. He seems to bring his "A" game home by simply being present and engaging with his kids and knowing who they are and what their interests are.

One day, the dad and his young son were in their front yard together. The dad was busy doing yard work while his son was very upset about something. The young son approached his dad, and the dad stopped what he was doing to intentionally shift his focus. He got down on one knee, looked at the boy, and said a few words. The exchange seemed genuine, gentle, comforting, and reassuring. The boy relaxed, the dad hugged him, and they both returned to what they had been doing. Had the dad just told him to stop, they both would've missed out on an important opportunity for understanding and connection. He connected with his son and strengthened the highway between them. This father and his children demonstrate a deep level of trust and connection that comes from the time the father has spent building relationship with them.

This kind of relationship building is foundational and it

will affect children and the way they form relationships with others for the rest of their lives.

As parents and children interact, they form connections to each other that mental health professionals describe as attachments. Researchers have identified four different types of attachment: secure, insecure, avoidant, and disorganized.[2] These different styles of attachment are characterized by the amount of emotional and trusting connectedness between two people.

Here are brief descriptions of how children with each of the four types of attachment think and feel about their connections with their parents:

- *Secure Attachment*—I trust you. I know that you care about me. I recognize that people are imperfect in their love. But I know you're doing the best you can with what you know and have. If you leave, I will be okay. I can still love, even when you're having issues. I understand that you might be able to love me or you might not, but I will be okay.

- *Insecure Attachment*—I'm not sure if you always love me. I need to cling to you because I might lose you. I can't be alone, because it means I'm not loved. Don't leave me. I'm worried that if I mess up or disappoint people, they won't love me. If you leave me, I will not be okay. Please don't leave. If you stay, I will be okay.

Make Every Day Count

At Focus on the Family, we believe there are five simple ways to make every day count in your relationship with your children:

DINNER

Do your best to have at least one meal together each day. Dinner works best for most families. Our family also tries to squeeze in at least ten minutes for breakfast together on school days. Life is busy, but we all have to eat. Meals present opportunities for connection and refueling (mentally, emotionally, physically, and spiritually).

LAUGHTER

Find things to laugh about. Life can easily get serious fast. Laughter is truly a great medicine and connector. In fact, research supports the fact that laughter is an attachment behavior.[3] It helps bring us closer together. You can find great clean jokes to get laughter moving online or in our two kids' magazines (*Focus on the Family Clubhouse Jr.* for the younger kids and *Focus on the Family Clubhouse* for eight- to twelve-year-olds).

PRAYER

Praying for and with each other leads to awareness, caring, and compassion toward one another. Prayer aligns our minds in agreement with God and provides opportunities for closeness, intimacy, openness, and bonding with one another. God is ready to talk at any time. He desires unity and wants to give us direction along the way. Find frequent times to pray together.

TIME

The parenting years fly by and are quite busy. Carve out time to spend together. Spending time together promotes healthy attachment. How you spend your time shows your priorities. We all waste time, we all get distracted, and we all need reminders. This one is tough, especially with technology creating ongoing and never-ending conversations that interfere with face-to-face interactions and moments. This takes ninja-level intention and attention.

CONVERSATION

Conversation doesn't always flow. The more you know your child and do the other four exercises of making every day count, the more likely it is that you will have things to talk about. I have worked with many dads and sons who say they would love to have more frequent and meaningful conversations but don't know what to talk about. Find something to enjoy together. Find commonalities and interests. Take interest in each other's interests, pursuits, and dreams. Work toward having undivided-attention conversations. Being truly listened to leads to feeling important and loved.

- *Avoidant Attachment*—I don't always need you, but you may be useful to me sometimes. You might hurt me, so stay away unless I need you. I can do things on my own. I can't remember anything painful in my past and can't be hurt by others. If you leave, I will be fine because I don't really need anyone to survive.

- *Disorganized Attachment*—You hurt me, but I still want to be with you sometimes. Go away, but don't go away. I want to be with you, but I'm scared of you and can't trust you. I'm confused. I want to be with you and I don't know why, because you're not safe and you hurt me. I hate you and I love you.

The goal is to develop secure attachments in our children. You can do this by being a *noticer, builder,* and *connector* in your child's life. Building a loving, trusting relationship with your child takes time, intention, and love. It's quite possible to develop secure attachments with your children even if you've had other types of attachments in your own life. This will take some time of reflection on your part. Research each type of attachment in more depth to determine what your experience has been along the way. Consider with much grace and forgiveness how your relationship with your parents has affected your ability to attach as a parent. Thoughtfully consider what practices you'd like to bring to your parenting and what practices you'd prefer to avoid.

3. Boundaries

The first two levels of the Provision Pyramid, basic needs and relationship, develop trust between children and parents. The child learns to trust the parent and to relate to others. This trust gives the child security and an openness to boundaries. These two levels must be attended to first, in the early years of life. In the next two levels of the pyramid, loving parents build on this trust. Parents provide direction to their children as they begin to engage with the world and find their places in it. Parents help their children know what to say no to (boundaries) and what to say yes to (direction). Let's talk more about boundaries.

Lovingly set boundaries provide children with reassuring fences that offer structure, safety, and freedom from the lures of temptations and sin. The more children learn healthy boundaries, the more they are able to develop clear and consistent direction in their lives and feel secure. This helps them become contributors in God's Kingdom rather than consumers. Consumers are controlled by "what's in it for me?" and "this is unfair." Contributors are driven by the opportunity to give of themselves and are much more adaptable to and responsive to spiritual desires and direction.

Providing boundaries is truly a loving thing to do because limits help your children know how to navigate life. Our lives need boundaries in several areas:

You and Me Together for Definitely Ever

Several years ago, my wife and I watched a movie in which the characters used the phrase, "You and me together forever." I said, "Hey, let's say that with our children, because we will be together forever in heaven." So we started saying that, and it became part of our family culture.

One day my seven-year-old daughter brought me a silicone bracelet and said, "Dad, you need to wear this until you die." Unfortunately, the bracelet didn't fit, so I twisted the bracelet and made it a ring for two of my fingers. Her face lit up, and we decided that it could be a together-forever ring.

She asked if there were rings like this that dads could buy to wear as a reminder of being together forever with their daughters.

- *Time*—What are we involved in? Where are we spending our time? How are we helping our kids make wise decisions with their time?

- *Relationships*—Whom do we spend time with? How do we treat others? How do we allow others to treat us? How do we maintain relationships?

- *Decisions*—What does our decision making look like? Do we invite God into the process? Do we consider the investment of time and money as we make decisions?

- *Space*—When do we need rest? Do we take time to be with people and time to rest and be alone? Do we have a place that is our own? How do we teach kids about respecting people's space, physically and emotionally?

- *Expectations*—What are we expecting from others? What is being expected from us? What do our children learn from how we deal with expectations?

- *Demands*—What demands have been placed on our time, talents, and attention? What demands on time, talents, and attention are we placing on others?

- *Morality*—What do we believe to be right and wrong? Do we model limits based on Scripture? What limits are necessary as a moral compass develops and grows in our children?

This is not an exhaustive list, but it gives you the idea that boundaries are about more than discipline and correction. They are also about wise decision making—discerning and choosing between ideas and practices that benefit us or harm us.

Using the state, city, and roads illustration makes it easy to see the need for limits. The state, each city, and the roads all need appropriate limits in order for everything to function without chaos and to provide freedom.

I researched it and told her no. She decided that we needed to make them. I laughed, but she was serious. It began quite an adventure for us as I drew up the specs for a silicone ring to go over two fingers with a knot in the middle. My family had lots of fun designing the rings and getting them manufactured. I continue to wear the rings and frequently get asked about them.

Find something you can wear or make together or do together to symbolize the reality that your relationship can last for eternity. You don't have to wear rings. My children and I also have a hand gesture that we can do from a distance to remind us that we will be together for *definitely* ever, because of God's reassurance of eternity together with Him. You can provide some kind of reminder such as a handshake, facial expression, note, or phrase to serve as a reminder of eternity together, *no matter what.*

In our lives, having limits is not about creating happiness but about showing respect and love for one another. Having boundaries helps us grow into the people God intends for us to be.

4. Direction

If you have provided for your child's basic needs, connected through an investment in relationship, and provided boundaries, your child will be ready for meaningful direction and guidance from you. This step takes parents into a deeper steadfast love for their children. It involves exploring and developing a life vision, a mission, spiritual understanding, and focus. However, in order to do this, it is helpful for you to be open to imperfection and failure. What I mean by this is that kids need to be guided through the questions, mistakes, and difficult moments in life with grace and relationship. Your children will have plenty of moments of weakness, failure, and difficulty. Patiently and intentionally influence, encourage, and contribute to them as they seek answers and direction.

Some of my greatest moments of growth have been when I failed, made poor decisions, and made it through difficult moments because I had to either crumble or become stronger. The way my parents handled the three sections at the bottom of the Provision Pyramid helped me have the foundation to receive meaningful direction from them during these difficult and confusing times.

It can be tempting to rescue our children in their difficult moments. But as difficult as it is, it is not helpful to shelter our kids from failure, pain, difficulty, and struggle. This stage is necessary in preparation for reaching the tip of the pyramid, which is understanding our own identity in Christ and our ultimate dependence on His perfect, steadfast, never-ending love. We need to work toward helping our kids persevere as they experience steadfast love, find purpose, and gain resilience.

I remember the father-child trip to the Ansel Adams Wilderness I took with my son a couple of years ago. We enjoyed a few days of connection, reflection, and direction with other participants, the guides, and God. It was a powerful adventure with my son. One of the activities involved using a map and compass to find our way to a freezing-cold lake along with other dads and sons. On the map it looked straightforward and easy, but once we were in the middle of

Chess Activity

Play two games of chess with your child. Play one game with rules and the other without rules. Compare the games. Ask your child which one was more fun to play. Discuss why rules are important. Here are some questions to consider:

Without rules, how do you know that the participants have played fairly? Without rules, how do you solve disagreements between players? Without rules, how do you know who won the game?

Read Judges 21:25 with your child and discuss what happens when there are no defined limits. It's a mess! Having no limits in life creates chaos and promotes selfishness. Healthy and biblically based boundaries provide and invite respect to the relationship.

the expedition and experience, it was a different story. We were confused, lost, and in need of constant redirection as we veered off the trajectory toward the destination.

The same is true of life. Leading our lives toward a destination seems straightforward until we're actually in it. We read Scripture and have great intentions until life splashes us in the face. Experiencing this adventure with a group of dads was a great illustration for me as I come alongside my son. I picture God as the ultimate guide whom I need to connect with along the way as my son and I seek to find and follow His path. However, in order for the journey to go well, we will need basic provisions, relationship, and boundaries. We will benefit from trust, relationship, safety, connectedness, and redirection as we seek clear direction.

There are a few things you can do to help provide direction to your children.

Pray Faithfully

As a family, take time to listen to God. Discuss the idea of thirsting for God and confidently bringing your needs and concerns to Him rather than being anxious. Provide time for family members to pray individually. Come together after a few minutes and give anyone who wants an opportunity to share about what God is telling him or her. You may want to write down your family's ideas. I have a listening book, which is a small journal I use to write things God may be telling me. It's helpful to review these ideas frequently.

Write Notes to Your Children

The notes could be inspirational quotes, jokes, words of encouragement or love, or observations of who God has created them to be. These notes could also be a picture illustrating a thought or just a simple reminder of love. Reminders of genuine love are like a refreshing glass of water on a scorching-hot day.

Model Asking Reflective Questions

Help your children learn to look inward rather than outward. This gives your children the wisdom that comes from understanding themselves. It will help them hear the voice of God rather than being swayed by the crowd. You can ask each other these questions:

- Whom do I compare myself to and why?
- What makes me angry? Happy? Sad?
- What is important to me and why?
- What is the most life-giving quality about me?
- What gives me a sense of satisfaction and why?
- What is God doing in my life?
- What gives me a sense of security and self-worth?
- Do I feel lonely? Why?
- What makes me feel stressed? How do I handle stress?
- What have been some of my favorite and least favorite days of my life so far?

Serve Others and Talk about the Gift of Serving Others

Discuss the many Bible verses about "one anothering" in Scripture. Here are a few about love:

- Be at peace with one another (Mark 9:50).
- Love one another (John 13:34; 15:12; 1 Thessalonians 3:12; 4:9; 1 Peter 1:22; 1 John 3:11; 4:7).
- Through love, serve one another (Galatians 5:13).
- Be devoted to one another in love (Romans 12:10).
- Bear with one another in love (Ephesians 4:2).

Write a Family Mission Statement

This may not be everyone's thing, but it is definitely effective when implemented well. A mission statement could be as simple as *We will develop trust, direction, and purpose in our home through steadfast, loving relationships with God and each other in order to freely and effectively serve together in God's Kingdom.*

As we find direction in our lives and conquer adversity, we learn about purpose and identity. We learn about ourselves through our relationships: Who has God created me to be? Who has God said that I am to Him? You have the privilege of coming alongside your children as they discover who they've been created to be and for what purpose.

5. Identity

The previous four levels serve as a foundation for developing a healthy sense of identity as a loved child of God. I believe many kids feel empty today. They desperately need to know that they are deeply loved and that their lives have unique design and purpose. That's why it's so important for parents to comprehend that their work of steadfastly loving their children has an ultimate goal. As the lower levels of the pyramid are completed and the final point of the pyramid takes shape, your child will be coming to an understanding of what it means for him or her in particular to be a child of God. Your child will be discovering what his or her unique design and purpose are in the Kingdom of God. This is the culmination of all we do as loving parents.

Love in parenting is best when it is structured according to how we are loved by our Abba Father—such love is steadfast rather than conditional. This kind of love creates the fulfillment kids are craving and not finding in our culture. Genuine trust, meaningful direction, and lasting purpose are noticeably absent in the fabric of today's society. And it's far too common for Christian homes to conform to the world in this area. In other words, we are deficient in steadfast love in our homes. Let's bring back our identity as children of God with a rich inheritance in Christ!

FROM GENERATION TO GENERATION

Being a parent has stretched the limits of my energy, patience, love, worry, dependence on God, busyness, and attention. In Deuteronomy 6 and 11 and in Psalm 78, God makes it clear that we show love as parents by passing on His teachings, commandments, and love from generation to generation.

ACTIVITY

Masks

Discuss with your child the idea that we all wear masks that hide our true identities. Explain that others often do not see us for who we really are—they misunderstand us or fail to get to know us authentically. Talk about how others' expectations and our own fears can cause us to wear a self-protective masks—to represent ourselves to others differently than we truly are. Invite your child to share how this has been true in his or her life.

Then to represent this idea, have your child make a mask as beautiful as possible using whatever materials you have on hand. Have your child write on the mask, or on a sheet of paper, how others see him or her in ways that aren't true.

Next explore what God says about your child in Scripture:

John 15:15: *Through Christ, we are God's friends.*

Romans 8:17: *Through Christ, we are God's heirs.*

Romans 8:38-39: *Absolutely nothing can separate us from God's love.*

2 Corinthians 5:17: *Through Christ, we are new creations.*

Galatians 3:26: *Through Christ, we are children of God.*

Ephesians 1:5-6: *Through Christ, we are adopted into God's family.*

Ephesians 2:10: *We are God's workmanship, created by Him to do good works that He has already prepared for us to do.*

1 Peter 1:18-19: *Through Christ, we are ransomed.*

1 Peter 2:9: *We're a royal priesthood, a people for His own possession.*

Have your child make a picture frame, using materials you have on hand. Write verses and messages on the frame regarding who God says we are as part of His family and Kingdom.

The picture frame represents our identity in God's Kingdom. He has formed us and continues to build us as His children. He is the one revealing the picture of our true identity. We can hide behind our masks or we can patiently and honestly embrace the masterpiece that God continues to make of us as we are perfected in Him. Remember, we are all under construction and we need to live in authentic "one anothering" relationships. That is God's design.

Build a fire together in a fire pit. Talk about your child's mask and picture frame. Together decide which one goes in the fire. If your child spent a lot of time on his or her mask, he or she will most likely hesitate, which is great! The same is true when it comes to our trying to create and maintain our own identities. We are designed to serve and to love through who we are and what we do.

Part of our role as parents is to introduce our kids to a loving God who wants them free from the allure, the grip, and the consequences of sin. God cares deeply for His children and illustrated the ultimate economy of deep, steadfast love: sacrifice, pain, suffering, and death for the other. God provides—and we get to share in the joys and strains of provision for our kids—steadfast love.

KEY TAKEAWAYS
CHAPTER 5

STEADFAST LOVE

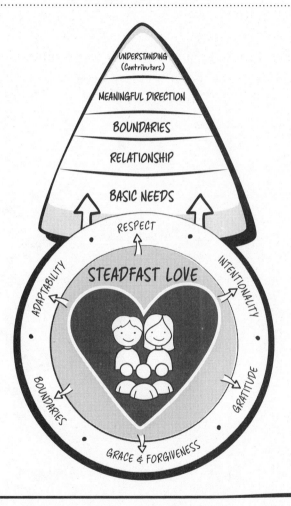

UNDERSTANDING
(Contributors)

MEANINGFUL DIRECTION

BOUNDARIES

RELATIONSHIP

BASIC NEEDS

RESPECT

STEADFAST LOVE

ADAPTABILITY

INTENTIONALITY

BOUNDARIES

GRATITUDE

GRACE & FORGIVENESS

BIG IDEA

○ Love is balancing warmth & limits, sensitivity & guidance.

○ The ultimate form of steadfast love includes taking care of ourselves so that we can be a gift to others.

○ Becoming a parent transforms us at a biological level; our brains begin to change as does our way of looking at the world.

CHAPTER 6

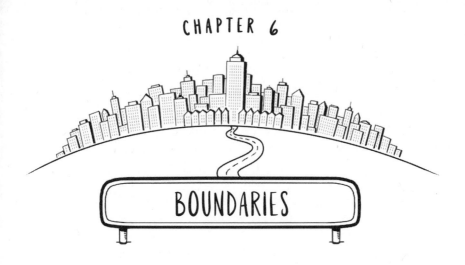

BOUNDARIES

You get what you tolerate.
–HENRY CLOUD

How can a young man keep his way pure?
By guarding it according to your word.
–PSALM 119:9

SEVERAL YEARS AGO, when my wife and I were having our house built, we walked the lot and looked at the property we had purchased. The property stakes were the initial markers for the boundary lines. As the house was built and the landscaping was developed, several boundaries were developed and established along the way. Each room had walls, windows, and doors to develop boundaries inside the house.

In our yard, we installed edging to keep the grass from going into the mulched flowerbeds, and we built raised beds to contain the raspberry bushes and keep rocks out of the vegetable garden. We also installed a fence around our whole backyard to keep our small dogs and kids in and to keep out-siders from coming into our yard uninvited.

All of these boundaries in our home and property served a variety of purposes. In every area, these boundary lines kept things that belonged inside the boundary and kept things that didn't belong outside the boundary. The boundary lines also defined the purpose of a particular area: The raised beds were for raspberries and flowers, and dogs weren't allowed there. The boundaries we established for our property enhanced safety, order, beauty, enjoyment, and functionality.

In a similar way, the boundaries of life provide structure to our world so that we accomplish what needs to be done in ways that are safe, healthy, and appropriate. Setting appropri-ate, healthy boundaries for our children is both a necessary and a loving parental responsibility.

There are many different kinds of boundaries.

Boundaries could mean the limits of a child's develop-ment. A three-year-old is capable of certain things cogni-tively, emotionally, and physically. But there's a natural limit to what can be expected of a three-year-old. A six-year-old and a twelve-year-old are developmentally capable of dif-ferent things.

Boundaries could mean the limit of one's abilities. Someone might be skilled at basketball but not be a good long-distance runner. Someone might find math easy but writing difficult. Someone might find drawing a natural expression but can't ever master a musical instrument.

Boundaries could mean the limits I place on others'

treatment of me and the limits of what I'm willing to do for others in order to promote respect in healthy relationships.

All of these kinds of boundaries are important, and each type of boundary has implications for parents. However, for the sake of this discussion, we'll focus our conversation primarily on the boundaries that parents place on their kids for both their protection and their healthy development. These boundaries help kids stay safe, learn right from wrong, and develop maturity and responsibility.

Setting healthy boundaries requires discernment, wisdom, courage, and relationship. Boundaries determine both limits (the lines we should not cross) and expectations (the results we desire in a given situation). And while there may be consequences for crossing a boundary, there is also great freedom within the boundary. Boundaries are implemented well when there is a willingness to consistently teach, correct, guide, stop, and start what is most helpful for yourself, your spouse, and your children.

Most parents would say that setting boundaries is difficult for them. In fact, out of the seven traits, this is the trait most parents consistently score lowest on in the Seven Traits of Effective Parenting Assessment. Why? It's because setting and consistently enforcing boundaries is hard! It takes a lot of energy, awareness, and attention. It takes continued effort that goes against children's natural tendencies to test boundaries. When the parent says, "Don't touch the hot stove," the child's natural desire is to touch the stove because human nature urges us to make sure those boundaries are real. Our natural response is driven by our curiosity about why those boundaries exist. We have to test things for ourselves. We push against the limits we feel others have imposed on us.

And yet, boundaries are needed and desirable. Without boundaries, civilizations collapse, families struggle, companies fail, and people get hurt. None of this is accidental. It's all part of God's perfect design.

A BIBLICAL FOUNDATION

God is the definer of boundaries and limits. His creation is built on boundaries and limits. Consider Proverbs 8:29: "He set for the sea its boundary so that the water would not transgress His command, when He marked out the foundations of the earth" (NASB). All of creation is orderly—it works according to the rules God established.

God has given people the boundaries that will provide freedom emotionally, mentally, and spiritually. God gave Adam and Eve the entire Garden, and they were free to enjoy it to the fullest. They were given just one boundary, just one rule, and they broke that rule. Scripture provides example upon example of both victories and defeats at the boundary lines. The stories of Cain and Abel, Joshua, Moses, Noah, Samson, David, Solomon, and so many more all show us the struggle that takes place at the boundary lines of life. Sadly, the Israelites had a continuous struggle with boundaries as they tried to follow God. Many times they found themselves wandering, enslaved, divided, and rebellious.

And we're just like them. Judges 21:25 says, "In those days there was no king in Israel. Everyone did what was right in his own eyes." This is often our experience too. We struggle to live within the boundaries God gives us. Why is this? It's because our natural tendency is to build boundaries from the outside in to control our behavior, rather than the way God has instructed us, which is building boundaries from the inside out, to train and shape the heart toward love and connection. You see, God's laws and commandments were always about training the heart and building the soul—they were never meant as a means of people control.

I realize that young children do learn boundaries from the outside in, but that is only the introduction. The real growth happens as children internalize the principles that undergird the boundaries we set for them and mature in their understanding and self-discipline. This is how we all come to have boundaries from the inside out. So when the early "why" questions come, take time to help your child understand the reasons for the boundaries.

In Psalm 119 David writes of his love for God's commandments and the lifesaving benefit he has received from them: "If your law had not been my delight, I would have perished in my affliction. I will never forget your precepts, for by them you have given me life" (vv. 92-93). In the same psalm, David expresses the view that God's commands have shown him the way—they are a "lamp to my feet and a light to my path" (v. 105). He writes that God's commands have given him freedom, not restriction, saying that there is room

The $1-per-Minute Technique
During a car ride, my son and daughter found themselves at a standstill in resolving a disagreement. They were failing to respect each other, and they were crossing boundaries our family has set regarding how we speak to one another. I had listened to their frustration escalate for several minutes. I sought God's wisdom to discover the lesson my kids needed to learn.

Finally, I said, "You guys get one minute to figure out a win-win resolution or you will be hiring me for $1 per minute to help you resolve the issue. Whoever does not participate in the compromise and resolution will be the one in charge of the bill, so that could be one or both of you." Within that one minute, they decided

to run in God's commands (v. 32). Isn't this what we want for our children—to see God's boundaries as beneficial to them, coming from His deep love for them? Remember that it took several lessons for David to come to this conclusion.

God gave us His Word as a relationship-, life-, and soul-building tool. The more we step away from it, the foggier boundaries become. Boundaries have to be intentionally built at the soul level, not just the behavioral level, and God is the Master Architect of the soul.

If you look at the concept of boundaries through the eyes of God and His desire for love and relationship, you will gain wisdom in developing a solid foundation and framework for boundaries and limits in your own life and in your family's life. However, our sin nature, personality differences, emotions, habits, behaviors, and limited time all contribute to challenges in this area, which is why God's presence in your life and home is critical to discerning the best boundaries for your home.

Let's explore several dynamics that affect the boundaries for your household. We'll start by looking at the three most common parenting styles. These were first introduced by Diana Baumrind in 1971.[1]

PARENTING STYLES

Do any of these sound familiar?

"That's not fair!"

"John gets to watch as much as he wants!"

"Ronnie got a phone. Why can't I have one?"

"I'm tired!"

"Why do I have to do it?"

"Why can't I?"

"Why can't I watch R-rated movies?"

"Can you just give me another chance?"

"When can I date?"

"Can I stay out until two in the morning?"

to work together toward a resolution.

In the years since then, I've earned very few dollars in these situations. My kids have learned the lesson of moving toward resolution rather than trying to get their own way. I've taught this technique to families I counsel as well. The important components are consistency, respect, and follow-through. Your kids need to see that you will actually intervene after one minute and begin charging $1 per minute thereafter until a mutually acceptable resolution is reached. Remember that your goal is not necessarily for both kids to be happy. The goal is to help your kids recognize that there's more than one person with desires, wishes, opinions, thoughts, and emotions.

Developing Internal Motivation: A Parent's Dream

Most personality types can be motivated by rewards, praise, attention, and recognition that come from the outside. However, the goal is for your children to be motivated from the inside, including when it comes to respecting boundaries.

It is easy to see motivation from the outside, but internal motivation is more difficult to see and to develop. Organizational theorists Thomas Malone and Mark Lepper identify and define the following internal motivations:[2]

Challenge—Pursuing something that is difficult, but attainable.

Curiosity—We love fences and considering what may be on the other side. When we hear no, curiosity says yes. We love to learn about certain things.

"Why can't I listen to that
   music? It has a great beat."
"Why can't I vape? It's not that
   bad for your health."
"Why can't I smoke marijuana?
   It's legal in some states."

As parents, we frequently hear remarks like these from our children. These kinds of comments indicate that our kids are not so sure that they agree with or want to comply with a boundary we've set. As parents, we choose how we respond when our children test the boundaries we've given them. In general, parenting styles affect both how we set boundaries and how we respond when our kids challenge the boundaries or cross them.

Authoritarian (Demanding) Parenting

Demanding parents react strongly, asserting their authority and control when children are at the edge of the boundaries. These parents believe it is loving to be strict and to lead children toward unchallenged and uncompromising compliance.

Boundaries are developed through the use of verbal or physical force, and high expectations are placed on the child. The parent wants immediate compliance and finds value in kids who are respectful and obedient and who don't make mistakes. The focus is control and perfection driven by fear of losing authority, control, or respect. This can be considered the military approach to parenting—a lot of order with inconsistent or distant relationship. Authoritarian parents would say, "Boundaries must be enforced and must be respected and followed."

Authoritative (Balanced) Parenting

Balanced parents are careful about the boundaries they place. They listen and respond to their children. These parents take the time and difficult road of balancing both control and freedoms. They can be considered the "seven traits" parents. They aren't afraid to place boundaries where they are needed for the safety and growth of the child, and yet they

Control—This provides security and power.

Fantasy—Imagination can take us places our minds normally do not take us. We love to explore new places with our minds.

Cooperation—People love the experience of true cooperation and are highly satisfied along the journey.

Competition—It feels great to win. Winning gives us a sense of power, strength, accomplishment, and value.

I have added these internal motivations:

Gratitude—This helps us feel the peace we need to engage and be present. It helps us pursue relationship and life. It fuels respect for moments and people.

Purpose within God's Kingdom—When we know in our souls that we are part of God's incredible and grand story, it fuels our passions and pursuits.

How can you develop and encourage some of these as you continue establishing boundaries in your home?

also provide room for their children to experience failure and learn from it. The focus is growth and development leading toward interdependence, respect, and connection.

Balanced parents balance limits with understanding, emotional warmth, and awareness. For example, if a child is tired and cannot get a chore done at the time he or she was supposed to finish it, the parent may graciously provide a different time to complete the chore, but still follows through on the expectation that the chore will be completed. Balanced parents learn to discern the difference between honest mistakes and intentional disobedience.

Research has found that kids with balanced (authoritative) parents were more satisfied with life and reported higher levels of well-being and self-esteem and less depression.[3] Balanced parents:

- are emotionally present
- provide limits
- have sensitivity—they make sense of what is going on with the child and respond with care toward the child
- are consistent
- are focused on growth and teaching rather than control or making the child happy
- listen
- communicate

A balanced parent would say, "Boundaries and limits need to be consistent and clear, and kids are always learning through relationship, guidance, and instruction driven by grace and understanding." The goal is not to develop blindly obedient children—that is, children who obey authority without pausing to consider the ethics and higher authority of Christ. The goal is to develop wisely obedient children who learn to respect and discern. Kids need to learn to be assertive with respect.

Permissive (Make Them Happy) Parenting

Permissive parents hand the reins of control to their children, giving them the freedom to do whatever they want. The goal of this style of parenting is for the child to be free to explore, make mistakes, and be happy. Boundaries are seen as unnecessary, unloving, and restrictive. Some studies have shown that permissive parents raise just as many or more bullies as demanding, authoritarian parents.[4] Children raised by permissive parents tend to lose respect for authority and experience a higher rate of depression. In fact, many of them lack direction and become very unhappy with life. They feel that they *should* be happy but are not. Happiness tends to become their pursuit at the expense of relationship, connection, and the difficult work of character formation. A permissive or passive parent would say, "Kids will eventually learn. Life will teach them what they need to learn. Boundaries are learned through experience."

• • •

We all have moments in all three parenting styles, but typically each of us lands in one style more than the others. Working on developing the seven traits helps you land more consistently in the most effective parenting style, the balanced style. Talk with your spouse about the differences between your parenting styles and your understanding of appropriate boundaries for your children. Starting at her child's birth, a mom's brain shifts toward fearing danger and pursuing safety for her children, while a dad's brain is more focused on play, adventure, and physical interaction. It's common for moms to want their kids to wear their helmets when they're riding bikes and for dads to tell their kids not to worry about it. It's also common for moms to tell kids to be careful and for dads to help kids push the safety limits.

You and your spouse will need to collaborate, communicate, and negotiate the best boundaries for each child. But remember that children are not here to just be safe. You also want them to live full lives and to grow. Don't get stuck trying to get your way and control each other as parents. Appreciate your spouse's point of view, recognize the value of your different perspectives, and give your children opportunities to be challenged while also providing some level of safety and reassurance. This is a tricky balance, one that requires listening to and trusting each other.

PERSONALITY DIFFERENCES

Each family is a unique blend of countless variables. What one family values is not necessarily the same as what another family values. If you have more than one child, I'm sure you've noticed that what works as a boundary for one child may not be successful with other children in the same family.

One of the biggest factors in this is personality. As you and your spouse discuss boundaries in your home, you'll also need to keep in mind your family members' personality differences.

Personality is the initial filter we use to understand and interact with the world around us. You can view personality as the unique culture in each family member's city.

Many personality theories identify four personality categories and use a quadrant framework to arrange them and show how people in the various categories interact with one another. We all tend to have some personality traits from all four categories, but every individual tends to have one personality type that is most dominant. Let's use the basic four personality-type divisions to understand how personality can affect boundaries. You'll find more information about personality differences in chapter 7.

Leaders

Leaders are strong, bold, driven, hardworking, intense, and active. Leaders also tend to be controlling, inflexible, opinionated, bold, and in charge. They demand competence in whomever they are dealing with. They prefer organization and a fast pace.

Leader parents may lean more toward an authoritarian or controlling parenting style. They may forget to use encouraging words and may be quick to criticize. However, leader parents are clear about boundaries and limits in their lives. They are opinionated. They are comfortable with the

Marble System

Set a goal for the week as a family. Your goal might be about the use of technology, using words of encouragement toward family members, finishing homework or chores before dinner, or adopting an attitude (and habit) of service to others. Each time you notice your children pursuing the goal, put marbles into a clear jar. This is especially helpful with kids seven or eight years old and under.

Once the marble jar is full, which is hopefully at the end of the week, you can have a family indoor or outdoor campout or celebration. You could camp out and watch a movie in your family room with s'mores from the microwave. The idea is celebrating as a family instead of handing out allowance

word *no*. And they do not tend to care about what other people think. They are not looking to make other people happy. They are looking to accomplish an objective.

Leader children may challenge or question boundaries. They tend to exploit any inconsistencies or weaknesses in boundaries, limits, and authority. Leader children want control and responsibility. They are competitive. They want to be the best, and they sometimes thrive in being the ones who create the boundaries. Teach them to use their leadership skills to get a win for the family. From an early age, teach teamwork skills, self-control, and ways to build others up (this will take patience and persistence). Leader children benefit from lessons on humility, collaboration, teamwork, patience, and compassion.

Peacemakers

Peacemakers want everyone to get along. They are emotionally and mentally flexible, warm, sensitive, friendly, caring, careful, personal, sincere, and compassionate. Peacemakers want everyone to cooperate and work together. They are more relationship-focused and less task-focused than other personality types. Peacemakers tend to be more easily offended and are in less of a hurry than other personality types. Peacemakers value fairness over winning. They tend to be fair themselves but may sometimes carry more of the load in order to avoid making others uncomfortable or unhappy. They are happy being in the background and not having the spotlight.

Peacemaker parents tend to have difficulty with boundaries; they will sometimes move fence lines to make others happy. They may be more permissive or authoritative, depending on their level of maturity, confidence, and comfort with conflict. They may hold things in until they explode and may not engage in necessary conflict that helps the relationship grow. Peacemakers tend to say yes a lot more than they would like. They are uncomfortable with the word *no*

money or some other individual reward. This forms a family habit of celebration. It's important to celebrate victories together as a family as you work hard as a team toward victory. Make sure you clearly agree as a family ahead of time what the victory celebration will be.

and tend to neglect self-care. They can be easily offended and may avoid instead of repair issues in a relationship. They can be great listeners.

Peacemaker children will tolerate doing extra chores and are more vulnerable to being taken advantage of by others. Peacemaker children do not tend to operate from conviction and can get themselves into difficult social situations if they don't choose the right friends. They tend to lack opinion and clarity. Given some encouragement and instruction, peacemakers can become influencers and contributors, and they can help people feel welcomed and at ease.

Talkers

Talkers can be playful, cheerful, charming, spontaneous, restless, changeable, flexible, and social. They can be disorganized and inconsistent, but they enjoy relationships. Talkers focus on relationships over tasks. Talkers are active and can be highly energized by people. They try to make things fun and can have a lot of energy.

Talker parents tend to love conversation and need to learn to stop and genuinely listen to others. Talker parents can be disorganized and unclear in their boundaries and limits. They try to make things fun and can be swayed with negotiation. They prefer change to tradition and play to work. Talkers tend to avoid conflict and will verbally establish boundary and limit lines, but don't always enforce those lines.

Talker children love social time and will often overstep boundaries in social settings. However, they rarely get in trouble because they are charming, cheerful, and friendly. They are able to get special privileges and learn that boundaries are movable with a little persuasion. Talkers love social time and can easily get distracted in tasks that involve other people. They are fun to be with and can make tasks quite fun. Have them provide creative ideas for getting chores done. Given direction and training, talkers can be very influential and encouraging to others. When focused, they can get a lot done.

Thinkers

Thinkers tend to have high standards. They can be perfectionistic, dependable, prepared, pessimistic, inflexible, opinionated, and organized. They are black-and-white when it comes to boundaries. They love lists, details, clarity, charts, and tasks. Thinkers are the organizers and managers of tasks. Without thinkers, the world would be more chaotic. Thinkers are considered the strategists and behind-the-scenes brains for the execution of tasks and projects.

Thinker parents tend to make lists. They sometimes lack grace in boundaries because of their black-and-white filters. Thinkers have the mindset of "work now, and if we finish, we play later." Their minds have a difficult time resting and they have a tendency to be critical. They thrive in a structured environment and are great fence builders. Thinker parents can seem cold and overfocused. They may not listen if they are trying to accomplish tasks. It is difficult for these parents to rest if tasks and projects are left undone.

Thinker children may intellectually challenge and

question the reliability and validity of established boundaries. They love to be the ones who create or are a part of creating systems and lists. They are loyal and will follow and respect the established fences they agree with. They will have the expectation that others should also follow and respect the boundaries. Disorganization is annoying to thinker children and can create stress in their lives. Given some encouragement and direction, thinkers can be quite helpful in developing consistent, clear, and essential boundaries in your family.

• • •

Personality types are much more complex than this, but this overview will get you started in considering that personality differences affect how we perceive, manage, and interact with boundaries. The difficulty comes with the mix of personality types as families are striving to have relationship, accomplish tasks, and maintain boundaries and limit lines.

Several years ago, a peacemaker mom and talker dad brought me their extreme leader son. The teen had taken over the house. He was demanding and in charge. Both parents were frustrated and wanted to know how to manage their dictatorial doer son. He was strong willed, opinionated, physically strong, and demanding. However, both parents had provided the first two levels of the Provision Pyramid—basic needs and relationship—so there was a foundation of trust between them and their son.

We discussed the strengths of each personality type and the difficulty of mixing them together. The reality is that the mom and dad were great parents, but the leader personality of their son quickly exposed their insecurities and weaknesses. This is true of many parents. There are moments within personality-difference interactions that create challenging moments in parenting. We *are* different. Dealing with that can throw us off.

These parents and their son worked to discover one another's different personalities and how each one perceived situations. They learned to listen carefully to each other and form a joint perspective. The goal was also to understand one another and to create win-win moments for the family rather than overpowering one another and gaining control.

The leader son helped his peacemaker mom with recommendations on how she could be more assertive, clear, and consistent with him. The peacemaker mom helped her leader son learn how to be more sensitive, compassionate, and gentle with her in day-to-day boundary conversations and negotiations. The talker dad helped his leader son learn how to be more relational and less laser focused on competence, power, control, and success in sports. The leader son helped his talker dad to be more consistent and clear when establishing boundary and limit lines. Instead of being opponents on a battlefield, these family members became a team that worked together.

CONTRIBUTE, ENCOURAGE, AND INFLUENCE

Sometimes when parents think about setting boundaries for their children, they see their role as the lawmaker or as the enforcer. However, this sets up parents and children as opponents—the kids break the rules and the parents lay down the law. There's another way to look at your parental role as boundary setter and boundary keeper that is more positive and affirming both for you and your children. Consider that setting and keeping boundaries in your family is a way to contribute to, encourage, and influence your children. Through contribution, encouragement, and influence, you will guide your children toward relationship, safety, health, and maturity. This is ultimately the goal of boundaries in the home. Let's look at each of these roles in more detail.

CONTRIBUTORS

Think back to the state, city, roads, and highways illustration. Every city needs contributors who make sound investments of planning and capital to help a city thrive and grow. Contributors shape the city as they choose to fund certain projects and choose not to fund other projects. These decisions form boundaries—some projects are green-lit and are accomplished, and other projects are abandoned.

In parenting, the boundaries that you set and keep in your household guide where your family and your children place their focus, their time, and their energy. The payoff is in the future. Over time, the contribution of healthy boundaries guides and shapes the growth of your kids.

Contributors teach about motivation, values, and priorities in life. Think of how the boundaries you set for your family teach about good motivation, biblical values, and godly priorities. Take some time to reflect on the fact that God has contributed greatly to your life. Consider how God's boundary lines have guided your own growth. Use this example as you set boundaries in your own home.

The opposite of contributing is consuming. While the contributor spends his or her time and effort for the benefit and growth of others, the consumer is looking out for the benefit of himself or herself. Consumers demand to be pleased. Consumers expect others to give them time, but seldom give of their own. Consumers want to be listened to, but don't see the value in listening to others. Consumers ask for help but hesitate to help others. Consider how this applies to setting boundaries in the home—your motivation should be the benefit and growth of your children.

And don't forget this other aspect of setting boundaries: Teaching about boundaries and limits takes a large investment on your part.

ACTIVITY

Team Chore Cleanup
One of the biggest boundary issues in many families has to do with getting chores done. Finding ways to deal with this productively requires creative problem solving.

One family I counseled has taken the team idea to a different level! They worked together to design family cleanup T-shirts. When it's time to clean the house, the whole family puts the T-shirts on and gets to work. Then when the work is finished, they plan a fun celebration. Celebrations can be simple:

- Go to the park.
- Go bowling.
- Watch a movie together.
- Go out to eat.
- Go out for ice cream.
- Go for a bike ride or walk as a family.
- Play a board game.

ENCOURAGERS

Words of encouragement have the potential to build up and to motivate. Encouragers realize that words have the power to promote healthy and loving connection between people. This type of connection can lay a foundation for boundaries to be understood, respected, and followed. Encouragers are careful about the words they use with others. Their words are motivated by a deep and abiding love for the other person.

On the other side, discouragers have difficulty managing their thoughts and tongues. Now, I'm sure we've all experienced this on both the receiving end and the giving end. The words of discouragers tend to deflate or destroy and can take away motivation. Discouragers tend to notice what isn't done rather than what has been done. Discouragers rarely stop and celebrate—they are critical of others.

Words of discouragement tend to come out when boundaries are crossed and consequences are needed. It's easy to fall into the pattern of discouragement—especially when we are stressed. However, there is great benefit in training oneself to respond to these situations as an encourager.

For example, a parent could respond to a child by saying, "You clearly have lots of energy today. Let's figure out the best way to help you get some of that energy out." On the other hand, the parent could say, "Stop! You're driving me nuts! Why can't you just sit and play quietly?"

Can you see the difference? Our reactions to our children can be dicey because life comes at us at full speed, and we don't always have the luxury of time to stop and think. But take time before the moment hits to consider your words and how stress can quickly derail you from your ultimate goal, which is to lovingly guide your child toward maturity. Practice using encouraging words daily and you'll find that, over time, encouragement becomes a more natural response, even during moments of stress.

INFLUENCERS

As you invest in relationship with your spouse and your children, you have influence. The question is what *kind* of influence are you having through the example of your own daily practices? What you do and what you choose to consume influences the building of your own soul, and it also influences your children as they watch and follow your example. Remind yourself that your kids are watching the way you handle boundaries in your own life.

Your child might ask questions about the boundaries in the home, especially when they are toddlers or teenagers. See these questions as an opportunity rather than a challenge to your authority. It is important kids understand the *why* behind boundaries as David expresses in Scripture (Psalm 51; Psalm 119). Having this understanding will powerfully influence your kids because they'll better understand your values and your goals.

Positive influencers teach that boundaries are for:

- building relationships
- getting things done

- making places and relationships safe
- developing and building respect
- guarding the heart and mind
- showing love
- creating true freedom

In contrast, without healthy boundaries to guide them toward good goals, people tend to either be directionless and stagnant or they are drawn in and ensnared by negative influences. In other words, they are distracted. Perhaps without realizing it, parents become distractors when they see boundaries as unnecessary. Read Deuteronomy 6:1-9 together as a couple or family and discuss how remembering God's Word can keep your family focused on what's most important.

Due to technology, social media, and entertainment, there are many more influencers in kids' lives today than ever before. There is also a lot of potential for distractors to confuse and pull your kids away from the direction you'd like them to go in. I have no doubt that you've had conversations regarding technology use, social-media boundaries, video-game time limits, and entertainment decisions if you have children older than eight years old. These conversations require a lot of patience and investment of time and energy. They also require some preparation and modeling.

If there is negativity already brewing in the relationship, these conversations can become quite difficult and explosive. In order to have influence in your children's lives, you will need to have some patience and ask questions. The more you stay calm and the more consistent you are between the boundaries you place on yourself and the boundaries you expect your child to have, the better these conversations will go.

Each age and stage offers new freedoms and new boundaries. Listen, observe, and respond in order to be a positive and active influencer at each age and stage of your children's lives.

COMMON AND IMPORTANT BOUNDARY ISSUES

Parents universally struggle to keep consistent and effective boundaries in several common areas: sex, dating, technology, and entertainment.

Parents frequently ask me, "When is the best time to get my child a smartphone?" or "When is the best time for my child to start dating?" There is a lot of complexity in answering these questions. It really depends on the maturity and personality of the child and the relationship the parent and child have with each other. The goal, again, is leading your child toward the top levels of the Provision Pyramid, eventually leading to truly knowing what it means to be a child of God.

Sex

Parents need to start early with the critical teaching of self-control along with the specifics of God's plan for sexuality. Children who learn about self-control when they are young are much more likely to do well in their relationships. You can begin teaching about good touch, bad touch, good pictures, bad pictures, and influences from an early age. Help your child learn about honesty, responsibility, integrity, social justice, community, and identity from an early age.

I recommend you go through the *Launch into the Teen Years* video-based program (Focus on the Family, 2019) or something similar with your kids prior to the age of twelve to initiate important conversations around this topic.

Dating

What is the hurry? What is the purpose? Dating can be fun and it can be devastating. Make sure you think this one through. Dating isn't a game and definitely has an impact on relationship patterns. Dating is not bad, but is your child ready to enter the whirlwind? Dating can quickly distract a child. I told my son early on that he was on the bench until at least sixteen years old. We wanted to make sure he would be ready to treat another family's daughter with respect and care. Any girl that he dates may become someone else's wife. We have discussed that dating will need to have a purpose, and initially it is about learning to have patience, friendship, and laughter with a young woman.

My son and I have discussed the goal of being a positive contributor in a young woman's life rather than a consumer. In other words, what drives his desire and care for the young woman? Her growth and well-being? Her spiritual growth? Or what's in it for him?

My son is now sixteen and has recently begun dating. He had to ask the girl's father for permission to begin dating her. My wife and I worked with our son to draft a dating contract, and he is learning how to best manage his time, responsibilities, and attention. He has to go on group dates or with us during his first year of dating to establish a foundation of trust. My son recently decided that he wanted to purchase *Renovation of the Heart in Daily Practice* (NavPress, 2006) to read with his girlfriend.

Technology

Again, what is the hurry? Technology has become embedded in our everyday lives, but it is also quite distracting. Technology is not going away, but families can certainly decide what the best boundaries and limits are for their families.

Just because everyone has technology does not mean your family needs to have it, especially young children. In my home, our plan has been that our teens would share an emergency phone until age sixteen. At that point we will consider whether they have built trust and communication and are displaying mature decision making before getting them individual phones. Still, I realize that they will not be perfect and that there will be difficult moments and bumps along the way, but we need to make sure things are moving in the right direction before introducing such a powerful distractor into the mix. My son has seen the distractions and demands that technology brings. He knows that accountability and openness are important to maintaining relationships and smart decision making.

Entertainment

The entertainment we consume directly affects our beliefs, thoughts, and soul, and the boundaries we set as parents are intended to guard the heart and mind. I enjoy overseeing the

Great Resources regarding Technology and Entertainment Use

TECH Parenting is an acronym developed by the American Academy of Pediatrics.[5]

TALK to your kids about their media use and develop ways to monitor what they're consuming in media and technology.

EDUCATE—You can help your kids learn about marketing practices and the fact that entertainment rarely provides a realistic view of potentially negative and destructive consequences that can come from risky behaviors.

CO-VIEW and CO-USE media—Model healthy and appropriate use of media. Spend time learning about the various technology and entertainment options your children are interested in consuming.

HOUSE RULES FOR MEDIA USE—Clear and consistent limits are essential. Talk about the non-negotiable and negotiable limits regarding technology and entertainment. See focusonthefamily.com/phone-contract-sample.

Other Resources:

PluggedIn.com—Provides parents a biblically based perspective on current entertainment (music, video games, movies, streaming television, YouTube, apps), culture, and technology.

NetLingo.com—Provides information regarding the latest terms being used over text and is basically the dictionary for the internet. A great tool for parents as they navigate ever-changing online language.

Waituntil8th.org—A site empowering parents to wait until at least 8th grade to allow their kids to have smartphones.

Mediatechparenting.net—A seasoned educator offers information and helpful tips to parents and educators through a blog to help them effectively navigate the digital world as they teach and guide children.

Commonsensemedia.org—A comprehensive resource on media use for parents. They offer helpful research, articles, and advice regarding media.

American Academy of Pediatrics Media Plan—You can develop a personalized family media-use plan at healthychildren.org.

CovenantEyes.com—Technology to help families live free from the grip of pornography.

Plugged In department at Focus on the Family. The writers and editors are solid and talented Christians who want to help parents win at guarding hearts and minds in their homes. Don't be afraid to say no. There is plenty of entertainment that is not worth consuming and there is also some entertainment that is lots of fun to watch or play.

Start early and be consistent with the boundaries surrounding entertainment choices. This can be difficult when there are disagreements between parents on this issue. If you get stuck, don't be afraid to have a counselor help you determine the best boundaries and limits for your unique situation and family.

●　　●　　●

Setting appropriate boundaries requires patient directing and redirecting along the way. It requires wisdom and a lot of guidance from the Holy Spirit. Take time to pray as you develop, maintain, and adjust boundaries along the way.

As you reflect on what you have learned about boundaries, remember that it is all about relationship and growth. Boundaries and limit lines tend to bring out our weaknesses, but they are also great opportunities for personal and relationship growth. Pursue growth rather than perfection, connection rather than control. Take time to notice, invest in, encourage, build, and influence your children as you imperfectly help lead them toward a thriving faith in Christ.

BOUNDARIES

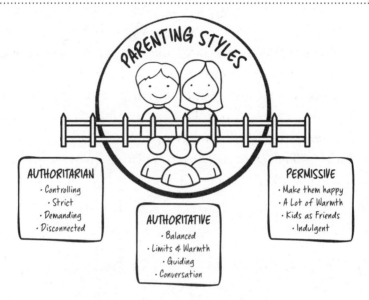

PARENTING STYLES

AUTHORITARIAN
- Controlling
- Strict
- Demanding
- Disconnected

AUTHORITATIVE
- Balanced
- Limits & Warmth
- Guiding
- Conversation

PERMISSIVE
- Make them happy
- A Lot of Warmth
- Kids as Friends
- Indulgent

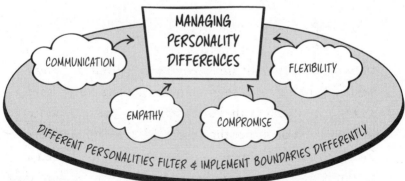

MANAGING PERSONALITY DIFFERENCES

COMMUNICATION

FLEXIBILITY

EMPATHY

COMPROMISE

DIFFERENT PERSONALITIES FILTER & IMPLEMENT BOUNDARIES DIFFERENTLY

BIG IDEA

- Without boundaries & limits, civilizations collapse, families struggle, companies fail & people get hurt. They are part of God's perfect design.

- Boundaries & limits must be intentionally built at the soul level & not just at the behavioral level.

CHAPTER 7

GRACE AND FORGIVENESS

God's grace and forgiveness, while free to the recipient, are always costly for the giver.
—TIMOTHY KELLER

Forgive us our debts, as we also have forgiven our debtors.
—MATTHEW 6:12

SEVERAL YEARS AGO, a tall, strong, and very angry seventeen-year-old came to my office for counseling. Greg (not his real name) was making excruciatingly poor life decisions and struggled severely with anger. He had become an expert at exploiting his mom's parenting weaknesses and negative reactions. The mom was desperate for help. The father had left the family when Greg was very young. In fact, Greg could not remember ever being with his dad. He said, "If I ever see my dad, I will punch him and kill him. I hate what he did to us and that he abandoned our family. My dad is a coward!"

A few weeks later, Greg's father contacted me. He knew that I had been meeting with Greg and wanted to be a part of it. That meant that Greg would have to sign a release-of-information form to give me permission to speak to his parents about his counseling. Greg, with a lot of hesitation, signed the form.

I asked Greg if he would ever be open to meeting with his dad. "I told you," he replied. "I hate him and I'll hurt him. I don't even know what he looks like. If he ever showed up, I'd be fine with meeting with him. I want to know why he abandoned us!" He left a crack open in the door to his heart. His anger was coming from hurt and confusion.

I talked to the dad over the phone about the risks. "I understand his anger," he said. "I would be furious too. I don't blame him for wanting to kill me. I am a big man and will be fine if he reacts physically. I just want to see my son and answer any questions he may have. I love him and regret all these years I have missed because of my own stupidity."

Greg said he had lots of questions for his dad and would be open to meeting with him but said he could not guarantee that he would stay calm.

The day came when the dad—a big, tall man—arrived to meet with his son. He was as nervous as a boy speaking in front of class for the first time and as excited as a child getting what he wanted for Christmas. He was full of grace toward his son and was willing to accept responsibility for his past decisions. He just wanted to be with his son.

When Greg arrived, he looked like a boxer waiting to

enter the ring. But I could see his nervousness as well. When Greg walked in, his dad immediately started to tear up. He stood and said, "Hi, Son." His son didn't say anything and sat down a good distance from his dad, glaring at him in hostility. I began the session with a time for questions and answers. Greg's first comment and question went like this: "I hate you. Why did you leave us?" His dad, with compassion, forgiveness, softness, nondefensiveness, and appreciation, said, "Son, it makes sense that you would feel that way. I would too. I love you and have thought about you a lot. I was scared and felt ashamed." He went on to tell his son the whole story of why he had left and not returned.

He said he left in order to protect the family. There were some things from the father's past that were putting the family in extreme danger. Once the threat was over, he felt too ashamed to come back. He didn't know what to do. He missed his family but did not want to hurt them. His son, moved by a glimmer of compassion and his dad's request for forgiveness, slowly and cautiously softened his anger toward his dad to the miraculous and God-driven point that he wanted to have some time in my office to continue talking with his dad alone.

Soon they were laughing together. Intentionally, I had not scheduled any sessions for an hour after theirs in case something like this happened. Well, God's ministry of reconciliation was alive and well. Grace and forgiveness danced in that room that day. I met with Greg for just a few more sessions. He continued spending time with his dad. His anger had been significantly reduced, his decision making had improved, and his life had experienced a reset.

Grace. It's an essential ingredient in the home. But sometimes we're too busy, too distracted, too strict, too permissive, or too indecisive. And our kids can be too hyper, too disconnected, too tired, too annoying, too intense, and too disengaged. Our imperfections require grace.

GRACE: BRIDGE BUILDING

Grace and forgiveness require a mindset of building bridges of connection rather than fences of comfort, self-protection, and control. God's bridge-building materials of grace and forgiveness are crucial for the vast array of imperfections in every home and relationship. Having grace toward someone involves trying to understand a more complete picture of that person's experience and point of view.

The three main steps of grace in parenting include focusing on your relationship with your spouse, understanding personality differences, and understanding the stages of your children's development.[1]

The Husband-and-Wife Relationship

The relationship between husband and wife requires large doses of grace and forgiveness. This is where patience and steadfast love demonstrated through grace and forgiveness are modeled for the rest of the family. Every once in a while, my children have witnessed some tense moments of disconnection between my wife, Heather, and me.

A few months ago, our family was traveling to the mountains for a short family vacation. My wife and I began to disagree about something. My adrenaline and internal emotional world turned to chaos. I did not feel heard or understood. Heather threw out the *always* and *never* words with some criticism, and my brain went out the window. The kids were in the backseat, watching us build a solid fence between us in the car. I decided I wasn't going to talk. There were several moments of tense silence until my son asked an unrelated question. He clearly felt uncomfortable with the large fence in our car. He wanted a bridge. So did Lexi. So did Heather. So did I. The bridge building at that point was up to Heather and me.

I told Heather I wanted to connect, and she responded with the same desire. We both felt unheard, misunderstood, frustrated, and hurt. We slowed down, carefully listened to each other, chose to forgive, and slowly let our emotions catch up with what we had decided. We weren't instantaneously eager to talk, laugh, and be with each other, but we replaced the fence with a bridge. We both slowly and emotionally walked across the bridge. The kids witnessed the realities of marriage: It's not easy, and it requires constant attention to maintain a bridge of understanding.

Personality Differences
People have always been interested in personality differences. There are countless personality theories and tests. But

to understand grace, all you really need to know is that each person filters the exact same reality through his or her own unique personality. These personality differences mean that we all handle the various situations of life differently from one another.

John Trent and Gary Smalley developed a quiz using four animals to signify the different personalities: lion, otter, beaver, and golden retriever.[2] I like to add one-word descriptors to these personality-type animals: lion = leader, otter = talker, beaver = thinker, golden retriever = peacemaker. And I also like to use four colors to represent these four personality categories because colors can be blended to create unique shades. These shades represent our individuality, the unique way in which we each express our personalities. We all tend to have some personality traits from all four categories, but every individual tends to have one personality type that is most dominant.

Yellow represents the talkers (otters). Talkers are playful, cheerful, charming, eager, optimistic, spontaneous, restless, and fun to be with. They have flexible mindsets, don't mind crisis, and generally prefer relationships over tasks.

Blue represents the peacemakers (golden retrievers). Peacemakers are sensitive, warm, compassionate, friendly, careful, loyal, personal, and people pleasing. They have flexible mindsets, tend to avoid and dislike conflict, and aren't overly opinionated.

Purple represents the leaders (lions). Leaders are independent, strong, bold, driven, curious, intense, active, and dominant. To a leader, work is play. Leaders are opinionated and have tendencies toward inflexible mindsets. Leaders desire control and don't mind conflict.

Light green represents the thinkers (beavers). Thinkers are organized, perfectionistic, dependable, prepared, traditional, and task oriented. Work comes before play, and they tend to see situations through black-and-white lenses. Rules, lists, charts, clarity, and structure are reassuring to thinkers.

These descriptions are basic, but they provide a framework for you to begin recognizing how each member of your family thinks, feels, and responds to life. This awareness can lead you to extend grace to your spouse and your children as you better understand them.

Interestingly, if you combine all four colors at equal strength, you get dark green—a color that represents growth in nature (grass, trees, and plants). Healthy growth in a family requires the grace to recognize, understand, and apply patience to communication and relationship in the home.

Grace, Forgiveness, and the Stages of Development

Many of us have kids in different ages and stages, which can make things interesting and challenging. There are some homeschooling families I have met who have six or seven or more children. In my counseling practice, I have met with several families trying to navigate every single one of the following ages and stages at the same time. Understanding the differences at each age and stage can help provide much-needed clarity.

Infants to Three-Year-Olds

Extending grace to children at this age involves understanding that children are learning a lot about their surroundings, needs, and wants. Become a student of your child. The learning curve is steep, and energy and sleep are rare commodities. If you begin with a lens of grace (understanding) when your child misbehaves, it will help you remain calm.

Extending grace to your spouse means understanding that he or she is doing his or her best with what he or she knows. Help each other be successful at parenting. Learn from each other and listen to each other. Forgiveness at this stage many times involves forgiving people in your past, your spouse's imperfect moments, other parents, extended family members, and yourself.

The sleep deprivation, noise overload, and chaos that come with children this age can make extending grace to your family unnatural. It's easy to say and do things in ways that you will later regret, especially if tension builds between mom and dad because of parenting-style differences. Work toward compromise and agreement in parenting styles. Have grace toward each other as you both try your best to parent.

Children at this age are:

- attempting to make sense of what they see, feel, hear, touch, and smell.
- figuring out who and what they can trust.
- constantly learning about the world through their senses.

- learning they have skills and abilities.
- figuring out consequences: "If I do this, then that will happen."
- crying and having outbursts as they learn how to pursue needs and wants. This is a great opportunity to teach, guide, correct, and redirect. The more you teach in this age and stage, the better the other ages and stages will be behaviorally and relationally.
- finding ways to be independent.
- needing to experience moments of failure and difficulty as they work on their skills and abilities.

Four- to Five-Year-Olds

Extending grace to children at this age means understanding that children are learning a lot about themselves, other kids, rules, and how to ride waves of emotions.

Extending grace to your spouse means understanding that she or he is working hard to teach, manage life, and connect. Be a team. It's easy to become critical of one another as disagreements surface. Also offer grace to other parents. Remember, you catch only a glimpse of their stories. Comparisons will only take you toward shame or pride. Try hard to stay away from these unhelpful emotions and extend grace. Grace will prepare you to forgive as "that wasn't supposed to happen" moments occur. Forgiveness at this age usually involves modeling forgiveness toward your friends, your spouse, your extended family, and your kids.

Children at this age are:

- quickly developing and learning.

- able to stay focused on a task for approximately fifteen to twenty minutes at a time.

- exploring through play.

- learning how to play and share with others.

- thinking and imagining out loud.

- experiencing emotional flooding and insecurities and could have intense temper tantrums.

- testing authority and limits.

- learning about obedience and disobedience, and their consequences.

- learning the critical and foundational traits of self-control and respect.

- asking lots of questions and needing parents to listen and respond to the questions.

- learning about taking initiative. Give them tasks to do and don't be afraid to let them be challenged and fail. Help them learn to manage frustration and disappointment as they learn they cannot succeed and win at everything.

Six- to Twelve-Year-Olds

Extending grace to children at this age involves understanding that children are learning a lot of new information about being liked and liking others through friendships. They may struggle with balancing loyalty to family and loyalty to peers. These seven years are filled with incredibly fast changes and opportunities to learn.

Teaching about forgiveness at this age continues to happen primarily by modeling forgiveness toward others such as friends, in-laws, extended family, your spouse, and other people. Forgiveness is also about having "resets" with your children when they are defiant, disobedient, or hurtful or when they accidentally break or ruin something important to you.

Children at this age are:

- experiencing a lot of changes in the brain. In fact, at around eight or nine years of age, children can develop a negative outlook about themselves and their circumstances. You can help your child see things from multiple points of view by asking, "Is there another way to look at that?"

- noticing sex differences.

- focusing more on whether something seems fair.

- tending to enjoy working in groups with their peers.

- testing limits and boundaries.

- starting projects that they don't always finish because sometimes they take on too much.

- trying to develop the skills they see in their peers.

- needing to be coached as they experience failure, disappointment, rejection, and discouragement.

- experiencing significant emotional and hormonal changes in preparation for adolescence as they enter the ten- to twelve-year-old range.

- becoming moody, impatient, and competitive. They may interpret failure as being inferior rather than as an opportunity for growth.

- becoming more anxious and worried. Help them learn to calm their minds through exercise, breathing, play, prayer, conversation, rest, or meals together. Each child will need to discover the best way to calm his or her own restless and anxious mind. Be patient as you discover what that is with your child. You are providing him or her with a tool that will be invaluable throughout life.

- beginning to notice and point out flaws, imperfections, and inconsistencies in adults.

- learning a lot about character, responding to authority, respecting others, and respecting boundaries. Work on developing consistent boundaries. Don't be afraid of questions about why you've placed certain limits.

Choose to see these questions as quests for understanding rather than challenges to authority.

- becoming impulsive and lacking awareness around eleven to twelve years of age. In fact, some experts believe that eight- to ten-year-olds can be more compliant and mature than eleven- to twelve-year-olds.

- seeking belonging and inclusion, especially when they reach middle school/junior high and can seem self-absorbed.

- experiencing more emotional extremes around eleven to twelve years of age.

Thirteen- to Eighteen-Year-Olds

Extending grace to children at this age means understanding that children are trying to develop close friendships, experiencing strong attraction and romantic feelings, and seeking to learn "Who am I?" It also means understanding that children are inclined toward rewards, risks, and freedoms.

Children's bodies are becoming more adultlike while their brains continue to grow. But they perceive themselves as being fully grown and knowing as much as their parents, if not more. Seeing children through grace means understanding that most of what kids are doing is about social, emotional, and personal survival rather than trying to overtly disobey parents or hurt others. Grace helps parents enter difficult and emotionally charged conversations peacefully, seeking to understand what children really want and need.

If you have exercised grace and forgiveness at each age, you have become more prepared for this sometimes-tumultuous age. There are several opportunities for forgiveness as teens wrestle through the many issues that face them at this age. Children at this age are:

- becoming more prone to taking risks.

- becoming more sensitive to the allure of rewards, especially the admiration and acceptance of peers.

- desiring novelty, which means they can get bored quite easily.

- focusing more on what peers think and say about them.

- longing to fit in or belong, without necessarily knowing the difference between the two. The difference is that in fitting in, children are forcing their way in by adjusting and morphing themselves. Children wanting to belong search for friendships where they can be themselves and feel wanted and connected.

- beginning to pursue specific interests.

- having miraculous, amazing, incredible neural pruning. This means that their brains literally become more specialized, depending on what they choose to pursue.

This is an exciting stage of life where kids can learn to become very skilled at something because their brains are ready for it.

- perceiving themselves as indestructible.

- tending to stay up too late, for a variety of reasons. Grace understands that a teen's melatonin does not tend to kick in until midnight or one in the morning. For older adults, melatonin generally kicks in around nine or ten at night. Melatonin helps us feel sleepy and tired. Many teens have busy schedules and want to relax and connect with their friends, who are also up at crazy hours of the night. They go on social media or the internet or play video games late into the night, which is known to wake up the brain and result in a very tired teen in the morning. You will need to be intentional about setting limits on technology, entertainment, and bedtime to help your teen make the best decisions in preparation for the next day. This can be a difficult and conflict-ridden limit. Enter the conversation with understanding but with limits and a goal to provide the best direction for your teen.

- not feeling cold as much as adults. Many teens wear shorts when it is snowing or just a light jacket when it is freezing outside. If they get cold, they learn to wear more layers. Just remember that they don't feel as cold as you think they feel.

- pursuing friendships as part of survival. They are developing the skills they need to live life without their parents. Their brains strongly react when they feel alone, lonely, or rejected. This can trigger a desperate pursuit of connection or a helpless resignation toward isolation and disconnection.

•   •   •

Cultivating grace between family members, despite your many differences, can lay the foundation for a family culture of forgiveness. With practice, you can have a home where grace and forgiveness are consistently offered and accepted.

Forgiveness is inseparable from grace. Grace helps shift the mind toward authentic forgiveness, and forgiveness provides freedom from emotional debts. As we enter moments with our kids using understanding and the pursuit of connection as the first steps, we allow forgiveness to be a part of the home. The combination of forgiveness and grace in family life aligns family members toward connection with one another.

Lisa Belkin does a great job providing an understanding of the complexities of parenting that require grace. She writes, "Contradiction is the fundamental truth of parenting. We want them to have self-esteem, but not pride. To master friendship, but thrive in solitude. To learn respect, but not blind obedience. To trust, but question. Be comfortable in their skin, but not preening. Be healthy, but also indulgent. Be independent, but still a part of us."[3]

Throughout my years as a counselor, I have met with several children and parents who have wrestled with authentic forgiveness. My daughter, Lexi, once asked me, "How do I know I have truly forgiven someone, and how do I know when I am truly sorry for what I have done?" These are difficult but important questions.

Grace brings the mindset and emotional freedom for authentic repentance and forgiveness. To forgive is the choice while grace is the love and empathy that helps genuine forgiveness take root. Eventually forgiveness chokes out the weeds of resentment, grudges, anger, and indifference.[4]

CONFESSION

God calls us toward ongoing confession to keep us in close fellowship with Him. But why? "We are sinners" is the simplest answer. But confession also helps develop a humble and grateful heart. It helps us see forgiveness as a gift rather than a right. Confession also allows for self-forgiveness, which may seem a little strange but is critical. Confession involves remorse over and ownership of what you've done, and it allows you to have grace toward yourself in the midst of your shortcomings as a spouse, friend, and parent.

A few years ago, my daughter and I had a great discussion about forgiveness. We were having fun dividing words for deeper understanding and decided to divide the word *forgive*: "for" + "give." We unpacked the idea of forgiveness as a gift. The word illustrates and confirms that there is an exchange. The word *for* indicates that there is something for another person. The word *give* provides the insight into the action. Something is given.

It is not always easy to practice grace and forgiveness. Researchers have found that more anxious, self-critical, and emotionally charged personality types tend to have difficulty forgiving themselves and others, while more flexible personality types are able to forgive themselves and others more easily and are more open to using grace in their day-to-day interactions.[5] As we discussed earlier in this chapter, personality is how we perceive the world. For simplicity's sake, you don't have to take a test to know if you are a more anxious, self-critical, emotionally charged, or flexible parent. Take a few moments of self-reflection or ask a friend or your spouse to give you some honest feedback to see if you can gain some helpful insights. Regardless of personality, here are some helpful steps to keep in mind when trying to develop the discipline of forgiveness.

Pray

Research supports the fact that prayer helps boost the ability to forgive. In fact, forgiveness researchers found that prayer enhances forgiveness, and forgiveness reduces stress and relationship issues.[6] Prayer is a central component in aligning our minds with God's will and heart. Whether you are praying with your spouse, praying for difficult people in your life, praying for people who have hurt you, or consistently praying for your kids, prayer can point your mind toward forgiveness and emotional freedom. What if parents got in the habit of praying when frustration, hurt, or disappointment showed up in their parenting? It can be a quick: "God, please help me. I need Your grace, wisdom, and patience right now." God freely gives to a surrendered heart!

Paul often referred to himself as being a servant of Christ. His surrendered heart gave him a natural flow of grace and pointed his mind toward forgiveness. Prayer moves the mind toward humility and surrender and away from control and demands.

Stop and Ask Questions

Like a detective, ask questions before drawing conclusions. Keep in mind that all people are under construction—we're all growing. Seek to understand the bigger picture. Rarely do people intentionally hurt, offend, or disappoint another person when the relationship is going well. Your kids, especially, are just learning how to do life. They are learning how to manage their wants and needs while learning about who they are and how they fit into this world. Many times, kids accidentally and unknowingly push buttons in us that they did not know existed. And *you* may not have known you had those buttons. There are certain behaviors and personality traits that can quickly get even the best parents off track. Seek to understand what is happening inside of you. And seek to understand what is happening to the roads connecting you and your children. Have you taken some time to bring grace into difficult moments?

Understanding

True understanding may involve confession, but it certainly also involves communication. Communication's central component is listening. Children soften when they feel heard—when they feel you "get" them. Take as much time as you need to explore the situation and understand your child. Lexi has said many times, "You don't understand." My reply is "*Help* me understand." I genuinely want to see what she is seeing and feel what she is feeling.

In Colossians 3:12-15 Paul says, "Put on then, as God's chosen ones, holy and beloved, compassionate hearts, kindness, humility, meekness, and patience, bearing with one another and, if one has a complaint against another, forgiving each other; as the Lord has forgiven you, so you also must forgive. And above all these put on love, which binds everything together in perfect harmony. And let the peace of Christ rule in your hearts, to which indeed you were called in one body. And be thankful."

What is said in this passage is powerful and convicting! Paul doesn't say we have a choice in forgiving. He commands that we forgive. I believe that forgiveness naturally begins to flow as we daily clothe ourselves with compassion, humility, kindness, meekness, and patience. That's because these virtues lead us to understand and have empathy and steadfast love for others.

ACTIVITY

Weekly or Monthly Family Questions

Several years ago, my wife and I attended marriage counseling, and the counselor gave us an assignment to take home. He said to ask each other several questions and write down each other's answers in a notebook. He told us just to listen to each other and write. He said to make it a safe moment to share. I thought it would be easy, but it wasn't. I wanted to defend, correct, clarify, and fix. Having to listen patiently, however, gave me insight into my wife's perspective. I chose to adapt the questions to use with my family and families I counsel. The questions are as follows:

1. What is going well for you?
2. What is not going well for you?
3. What is going well for us as a family?
4. What is not going well for us as a family?
5. How have you used grace and been a noticer, builder, and connector?
6. Whom have you forgiven?
7. Who has forgiven you?
8. What do you think could be done to make things better in our home?
9. What do you need from the family to help you feel more connected in our home?

Write down each other's responses in a special notebook designated for these meetings. Writing things down signifies the importance of the meeting. The meeting can be done while having milkshakes, pizza, root beer floats, tea, or any other favorite treat. It doesn't have to take a long time, and it is always best when it begins with prayer. In fact, prayer is a great way to begin aligning our minds with God's mind (Psalm 139:17-18) and moves us one step closer toward unity (Philippians 2). Keep in mind that you don't have to ask all of the questions at one time.

Speed Chess

This is a fun and quick (three to five minutes per game) way to play chess. Each person uses only eight pieces (four pawns, king, queen, and two other pieces of each person's choice) and gets three seconds per move. If the person takes longer than three seconds to move, the opponent gets to take the offending person's lowest-ranking piece off the board. The other rule is that each player gets two forgiveness moves per game, since the speed of the game leads inevitably to mistakes. When players want to use a forgiveness move, they have to ask for forgiveness and then get to take as long as they need to take their move back and choose a new move. The point is that they will not choose to do the

Resets and Do-overs

Time for confession. Did you ever press the reset button on your video game console when you were losing? I did. It meant I started over and used a different strategy. In relationships, resets and do-overs require humility and a lot of patience. Grace and forgiveness isn't about "winning" or "coming out on top." Rather, it's a matter of doing whatever it takes to heal a relationship. This is about bridge building and strengthening connections between us. Some families have drawn pictures of "reset" buttons and put them throughout their houses to remind family members to invite grace and forgiveness into their homes. Resets lead toward rebuilding trust.

Resets should be frequent in our homes. When Jesus told Peter to forgive his brother "seventy times seven" times (Matthew 18:22, NASB), Jesus was challenging Peter to have ninja-level patience, and He has given us the same challenge. Life is constantly coming at us, and things can pile up throughout the day. We may respond with quick impatience or even anger. Take whatever moments you can get, whether in the bathroom, in the car, or while walking, to observe your own emotional state.

A few months ago, while typing a paper for a class I was taking, I heard my daughter and her friend exclaim from the adjoining kitchen, "Oh, no!" This is not usually a good sign! My wife and I hurried to the kitchen to find a slow cooker full of soup melting and burning on a stove burner. The slow cooker had been sitting on the stovetop and Lexi and her friend had accidentally turned on the burner under it, rather than the burner under the pan they were using to make lotion. There was a cloud of smoke, and the house smelled like melted plastic.

After we cleaned up the mess, I decided to grab a glass and fill it with water while I stared out the kitchen window for a few tense moments. There were a lot of things I wanted to say that were laced with stress from

same move; it would be silly to do so. I have had teen clients play this and never use their forgiveness moves, even though they made careless mistakes. They consistently say that they forgot they had the forgiveness move, which is, many times, how life also plays out. This exercise can provide a fun way to discuss decision making and forgiveness.

other demands of that day. I wanted to ask, "Couldn't you see the cloud of smoke and smell the awful smell?" My mind was seething with frustrated sarcasm. I could not understand how a twelve-year-old and an eleven-year-old standing next to a stove did not notice a melting slow cooker.

As I stared out the window, I decided to practice the fruit of the Spirit—patience and self-control. I patiently waited for my brain and tongue to wrestle a bit. What eventually came out of my mouth was "That is quite an art piece." I knew it had been an accident. I also knew in my mind that Lexi did not mean to do it. Shaming her would not have helped her, me, or the situation.

We ended up laughing, taking pictures of the art piece, and getting a look at the makings of a slow cooker. I had never seen the inner components of a slow cooker before. My son also enjoyed looking at the circuit board and electronics that had been exposed. Had I not been patient, my first thoughts may have spilled out and hurt Lexi. I'm thankful God helped me control my thoughts before they got to my tongue. Sometimes we just need a few moments to create enough margin for our minds to calm down.

In that moment with my daughter and her friend, I had to dig deep to find empathy, which is a central ingredient to grace. For a few seconds, I looked at the moment from her point of view and remembered that I had to be forgiven many times as a child. We so quickly forget what it was like to be a kid and how much grace and forgiveness is required as we grow and learn. I believe grace and forgiveness truly give families resilience—the strength to keep getting back up, to keep trying, and to never give up (1 Corinthians 13:4-8).

GRACE IN BLENDED FAMILIES

Grace, empathy, and understanding can present special challenges for stepparents and stepchildren who get thrown together in the context of a blended family. An extra level of pain and misunderstanding often characterizes families formed by second and third marriages. In situations like this, children tend to look for someone to blame, and the new spouse or stepparent is usually the most obvious candidate. Parents who find themselves in this unenviable position can get things moving in a positive direction by modeling grace and forgiveness and by remembering that grace is all about understanding that each person's experience is different. Remember that the kids are not the ones who have chosen to be in a blended family.

Chain Analysis

Draw a chain of circles across a page. You may need two or three levels to complete all of the links of the chain. Each link represents a piece of what led to a specific problem. Write each progressive step that led to the problem and look for a place where there could have been a different decision, leading to a different result at the end of the chain. The chain analysis provides a helpful visual of how one choice can change the rest of the chain. It also helps pinpoint where forgiveness and grace are needed as part of the repair-and-reset process.

I love to have blended families use the "city under construction" illustration as a visual for discussion. The biological parents begin the family with natural connections to one another and build unique roads and highways over time. When the major cities (the parents) work together, the states do well. However, when the two major cities completely disconnect through divorce, the flow of traffic becomes much more complex and difficult. After a divorce, the entire state suffers and communication becomes more complicated. For the smaller cities (the children), this can create confusion, anger, and sadness. It is difficult for them to understand why the highways between the two major cities became impassable. They may feel that they need to connect to one major city instead of the other out of loyalty or admiration.

The disconnection between the two major cities often causes traffic (communication) to be redirected through the smaller cities. However, this rerouting overwhelms the smaller cities. It's a tremendous burden for the small cities to bear.

And then when a new major city suddenly shows up on the map, each smaller city has to decide whether or not to take the time and effort to build a road toward that city—a city they do not know. The small cities were fine with the major cities they were connected to originally. They didn't ask for a new major city to be constructed.

As a stepparent, realize that you can't rush in and quickly build brand-new expressways from your city to the smaller cities. You are stepping into a lot of history and emotions. The more consistent, patient, and understanding you are in these situations, the more likely a connection will take shape. Keep in mind that the connection may begin slowly at first.

The emotions that can spill out in this kind of scenario can easily trigger reactive emotions. For example, I once heard a child say, "He (the child's new stepparent) will never be my dad. I will never call him dad. My dad is my dad. He (his stepdad) has no right to tell me what to do. I liked him until he became my dad. I never want to be close to him, and I want my mom and dad to get back together."

Depending on the context, timing, and tone, this can all feel disrespectful and mean. Begin with prayer and adopt an attitude of grace. Try to understand everything from that child's point of view. Communication between you and the child must be safe—accept what the child says without reacting negatively or taking things personally. Offer much patient forgiveness and seek to make connection over time. The child will come to see that you are trustworthy and safe to connect with. Be consistent in responding, using the seven traits of effective parenting with prayer as your first step.

• • •

As you continue growing personally and in parenting, remember to begin with grace toward yourself, your spouse, and your kids. How do you respond to your spouse? How do you understand and handle personality differences in your home? Have you taken time to understand the age and stage you and your child are in together? Engage in this with your spouse as you both grow. Have you taken time to pray, stop, ask questions, understand, reset, and do over? There is plenty to forgive and be forgiven for each day. Let's be bridge and road builders together as we raise strongly connected families.

The best part of all of this is that God never said we needed to be perfect to express grace or practice forgiveness. On the contrary, grace and forgiveness belong to all of us, to each and every mom and dad on earth, no matter how imperfect we may be! Our goal as parents is to work grace and forgiveness into our everyday lives and continue growing in that direction as God gives us strength, patience, and discernment. It's hard to think of a more encouraging description of the parenting journey!

GRACE & FORGIVENESS

GRACE IN PARENTING

FOCUS ON

BRIDGE BUILDING — NOT — FENCE BUILDING

COMFORT
SELF-PROTECTION
CONTROL

← CONNECTION →

GRACE →

PRAY
STOP & ASK QUESTIONS
CONFESS & UNDERSTAND
RESET & DO OVER

AUTHENTIC FORGIVENESS

→ FREEDOM FROM EMOTIONAL DEBTS

BIG IDEA

- We are all constantly under construction
- Focus on resets, repair & reconnection in relationships
- Understand personality differences.
- Understand ages & stages of your child's development
- Be a road & bridge builder

CHAPTER 8

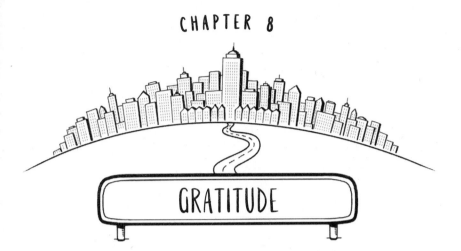

GRATITUDE

Gratitude is the healthiest of all human emotions.
The more you express gratitude for what you have, the more
likely you will have even more to express gratitude for.

–ZIG ZIGLAR

In everything give thanks; for this is God's
will for you in Christ Jesus.

–1 THESSALONIANS 5:18, NASB

GRATITUDE IS THE ABILITY TO appreciate what you have rather than agonize about what you don't have. It's the ability to focus on what's good in your life rather than on what's wrong. Gratitude leads to deep satisfaction and is expressed through genuine thankfulness.[1]

However, we tend to dwell on the small, niggling flaws in an otherwise-fulfilling life. We compare the mundane, messy details of our own lives to the high points in others' lives, and our own lives come up short every time. When we compare the cleaned-up, public-relations version of others' lives to the gritty reality of our own lives, we become dissatisfied.

How many times have you said, "If only we did devotions like they do" or "If only we could keep our house as clean as theirs" or "They get to go on trips to incredible places all the time, and we just stay at home"?

Social media has created a culture of comparison and dissatisfaction. We are curious about what other people are doing, and we are forever comparing to see how our lives, our families, and our children measure up. This comparison trap can even lead us to feel superior about our own lives when we become aware of the problems others are experiencing.

Our posting habits on social media show this most clearly. We all tend to post the brag-worthy, beautiful moments of life, but we don't share the failings or problems we experience because those less-than-perfect posts would make our lives look unsuccessful.

The problem isn't just with what we post, it's also with how much we post and self-awareness. A survey by *Parents* magazine found that 79 percent of parents believe other parents overshare on social media and only 32 percent think they themselves overshare.[2] Self-awareness is difficult, and we love positive feedback. People keep posting online because each time others respond or "like" their posts, the brain's reward circuitry kicks in and they get a jolt of the feel-good neurotransmitter: dopamine. In fact, several parents I have spoken to lament missing out on the overall experience in their own children's lives because they were too focused on letting others know what was happening. In other words, they were more focused on capturing the story and sharing it than actually living it and experiencing it. Parents post online to show how rich and full their lives are, but in reality they're missing out on the full, satisfying experience of the events in their families' lives. This does not lead us toward a spirit of deep gratitude.

It is not surprising that social media can quickly deplete our minds of gratitude and point us toward dissatisfaction. Social media does not present real life. It shows life with makeup, Botox, and perfect hair. Even kids have become great at posing with their parents in such a way as to show the idealized version of the events in their lives.

I will be the first one to admit that the impact of others in my life often gets ignored because my mind is preoccupied with other things. Life as a husband, parent, son, friend, vice president, therapist, and student is busy! But when I pause and think about the impact from my grandpa, my grandmas, my dad, my mom, my brother, my sister, my friends, coaches, neighbors, teachers, professors, and others, I am filled with gratitude for the unique set of connections God is using to shape me. Gratitude truly gives me peace in the chaos of life.

God tells us to not be conformed to the world but to renew our minds (Romans 12:2). He tells us to take our thoughts captive (2 Corinthians 10:5). He tells us in Proverbs 4:23 to guard our hearts. It's so important to keep our minds pointed in the right direction. Gratitude is a good way to focus your mind.

Take some time to reflect on this wonderful Scripture: "Therefore, as you received Christ Jesus the Lord, so walk in him, rooted and built up in him and established in the faith, just as you were taught, abounding in thanksgiving" (Colossians 2:6-7).

Notice the verbs in this passage: *received, walk, rooted, built, established, taught,* and *abounding.* What an amazing goal for my mind as a parent! There are plenty of moments when my mind goes sour and needs the refreshment of God's Word and the discipline of gratitude.

Do your kids see the mystery of the Holy Spirit in you? What I love about Colossians 2:6-7 is the reality of God working in me, the building process that God has used to establish my faith, and the realization of all that He has taught me along the way. This passage is about having gratitude for the imperfect and difficult process of becoming more deeply rooted in God.

The word for *humility* comes from the root word *humus.* Humus in soil provides nutrients and holds water, helping plants and trees develop deep roots. A key ingredient in gratitude is humility—realizing that there is always a lot to be thankful for every single day, including just being able to breathe, having a home and food, having the warmth of sunshine, and having a family. Even in the midst of chaos and difficulty we can be grateful.

Several years ago, when I was in my early twenties, I was at my new in-laws' home at a large family gathering. I was talking with my wife's uncle when suddenly the water I swallowed went down the wrong way. I had never experienced this before, and it was frightening. I couldn't breathe and I coughed like a seal. My wife's uncle didn't know what to do. The rest of the family watched in dismay as I gasped for air. I thought I was going to die. My mother-in-law (a nurse) came over and moved me around like a rag doll as she tried the Heimlich maneuver. She thought I had something caught in my throat. Suddenly, my throat calmed down and I could breathe again. I couldn't talk for a few minutes and was dripping with sweat. I had traumatized everyone in the room, including myself. I was immediately thankful just to breathe and be alive.

Like many others, I have had several more of those incidents with my kids and wife as witnesses along the way. These moments have been quite scary for them when they happen unexpectedly in a parking lot, at home, while driving, or while sleeping. Every time it happens, they stare at me in fear.

This has helped me realize how life can change at any moment and has provided our family with moments of gratitude for life itself. We tend to become most grateful when we think we may lose something. In other words, we don't fully realize what we've got until we come close to losing it.

While I was growing up, after a birthday or Christmas my mom would make us sit down and write thank-you notes. I have to admit that it was not my favorite activity; however, it taught me about pausing my life to be grateful and thank others.

I recently read about John Kralik. He wrote the book

A Simple Act of Gratitude: How Learning to Say Thank You Changed My Life. He decided to take on a personal challenge of writing 365 thank-you notes in a year—one a day. He wanted to focus outward and find reasons to be grateful each day. It changed his life. True, genuine gratitude results in well-being. God designed it to be this way.

There's a reason thank-you notes have maintained such a persistent presence in the story of the human race. We all want to be noticed. We all like to have our efforts acknowledged. We all feel good when our acts of kindness or generosity or sacrifice or hospitality leave a lasting impression.

Whom could you write a thank-you note to? What about leading your family in making a thank-you card for someone who has invested in your family? What about simply texting or calling someone today with a genuine "Thank you for . . ."?

THE DISCIPLINE OF CHOOSING GRATITUDE

"Give thanks in all circumstances" (1 Thessalonians 5:18).

There are plenty of circumstances that can derail us from gratitude regardless of our great intentions; however, we can learn to purposefully refocus our minds on thankfulness. In fact, I have heard some ninja-level optimists consistently and consciously redirect their minds toward gratitude despite very trying circumstances.

Here's an example from my life. I can quickly become stressed when I see our house messy and in chaos. So, over

GRATITUDE

the years, I have learned to work on shifting my mind toward being thankful that we have a house and things to organize rather than just focusing on the clutter. Believe it or not, sometimes I have paused, gone outside, looked at the house, and consciously redirected my mind toward gratitude for the house. There is always something needing to be done in our home, but it's also the place where my family lives, plays, learns, and loves. In chaotic moments, I am able to regain a sense of peace by getting a bigger and more complete view of the house for just a few moments. I open up possibilities and opportunities when I reset my perspective.

Don't get me wrong, though. Redirecting your mind to be grateful despite the stress of life isn't easy. I fully acknowledge the challenge of practicing it.

I remember our family hosting James Irwin, one of the astronauts to set foot on the moon, when I was a young boy in Mexico City. My parents knew him through events and connections at our church in Mexico. James Irwin is the one who encouraged my parents to consider moving to Colorado Springs. I remember that he loved to smile and laugh. One of the things I remember him saying during that visit is that the earth looked so peaceful from space even though he knew it was filled with chaos. He said he was filled with awe and gratitude as he looked at the earth from the moon. Perspective can change what we see.

Brother Lawrence learned to practice the presence of God by offering up thanks and praise while washing dishes in the monastery kitchen. And C. S. Lewis, in his spiritual autobiography, *Surprised by Joy*, tells us that gratitude was a key ingredient in his conversion to Christ. That's because gratitude always leads our thoughts beyond ourselves. Gratitude lifts us straight up into the presence of the One to whom we are indebted for every good and perfect gift (James 1:17).

Bottom line: Kids quickly grow up and you have the privilege of being a part of their lives. The more grateful you are for the beautiful, uncomfortable, challenging, imperfect, and fun opportunities parenting provides, the more peace you will experience even in the midst of life's chaotic moments.

THE GRATEFUL PARENT: FIVE KEY EXERCISES

Gratitude requires a constant redirection of the mind because we are prone to get distracted by the present moment, past experiences, familiarity, boredom, stress, and trials. I see it as a workout of the mind. Take a look at the suggested workout:

1. Be a Noticer

Nineteen-year-old Signalman Third Class Elgin Staples of Akron, Ohio, served in World War II.[3] He was aboard the USS *Astoria* near Guadalcanal when it was attacked by Japanese cruisers. Around two in the morning, Staples was thrown into the air and out to sea by an explosion on the ship. Staples was kept afloat by a rubber life belt. Both of his legs had been wounded by shrapnel.

Around six in the morning, the USS *Bagley* arrived to

help the survivors. Staples and other rescued survivors were then returned to the *Astoria* to help salvage the ship, but it eventually sank, pitching Staples back into the water. Around noon, the transport ship USS *President Jackson* arrived to begin a second rescue. Onboard the USS *President Jackson*, Staples noticed that the life belt that had helped him survive had been manufactured by the Firestone Tire and Rubber Company in Akron, Ohio, his hometown.

Upon his arrival home, as he was spending time with his family, Staples showed them the piece of equipment that saved his life. He was grateful to be alive and recognized the belt as part of his survival.

His mom told him that she had gotten a job at the Firestone Tire and Rubber Company to make some extra money while he was overseas. She was grateful for the opportunity of that job. Elgin quickly and excitedly told her that the belt had been manufactured where she worked. He also showed her a set of numbers he had noticed on the belt.

When his mom looked at the belt, she was filled with emotion. She told him the number was an inspector number and that the set of numbers on his belt was her inspector number. She had been the one who inspected the quality of the life belt that saved her son's life.

Staples's gratitude for life and his mother's gratitude for work provided strength in the midst of adversity.

Parents face adversity. Whether it is sleep deprivation, poor grades, illness, financial struggles, a loss of a job, loss of faith, conflict, or any one of a multitude of other trials, gratitude can provide perspective. J. P. Moreland and Klaus Issler wrote in *The Lost Virtue of Happiness* that life is filled with God's creative presence but we sometimes fail to see God's work in our lives or we dismiss it as coincidence.[4]

Take time to notice how God is involved in the details of shaping your story alongside the stories He is unfolding in those around you.

Be a noticer of:

- what God is doing in you, your spouse, and your children
- what you have rather than what you don't have
- contributors—those who have contributed time, effort, and money into your life
- encouragers—those who have spoken encouraging words or written you notes of encouragement along the way
- influencers—those who have said or done things that have positively influenced and pushed you
- God's creation
- God's response to your prayers
- what your kids and spouse do
- what God has for you to do
- the fact that every day offers something brand-new

A few years back, my son, Alex, and I went skiing. He got to skip a day of school, and I took the day off work. That day I felt genuinely grateful just to be out there on the mountain.

I had recently been through two hip surgeries and a shoulder surgery. All I could think about was how blessed and happy I was to be skiing at all! It had been several years since I had been on the slopes. At one point, I paused and waited for Alex, since he was just learning to ski. I marveled at the beauty of my surroundings: the clear blue sky, the pure-white snow, the jutting crags of the mountain peaks, the freshness of the firs and the pines. I was truly thankful for all of it, and to this day I remember how good it felt. It was like slipping out of the cold, sharp air and into the luxury of a steaming hot tub. There's no way to describe the effect that emotion had on my attitude and outlook that day! I realize these aren't common moments, but they're beautiful moments. The point is to pause and notice. Being a noticer takes intention and focus, but it's worth it.

2. Appreciate What You've Got

Several years ago, I was a school social worker and went on a home visit to assess what a particular mom needed in the face of the challenges she was experiencing. I can honestly say that the woman who answered the door was one of the most courageous and heroic ladies I've ever met.

Anita was a single, immigrant mom whose primary language was Spanish. She had married an American man who had abandoned her and her children. She cleaned houses to support her two children. Both of the kids had Down syndrome. One of them was also afflicted with severe physical problems due to birth defects. The doctors had foreseen these issues, and as a result they had counseled Anita to abort both pregnancies. She recalled sitting in the abortion clinic, waiting to abort her first pregnancy, when she decided that she didn't want to go through with it. She said the staff at the abortion clinic tried to convince her that it was the best decision, but she disagreed. She left the clinic and was eternally thankful she did. Her child was born with severe disabilities, but over time she noticed the incredible effect her child was having on her life. She thanked God for the child He had given her.

When I asked her how she was managing her difficult life, Anita gave me an answer that I'll never forget. She said, "I love my kids and each one is from God. I cannot imagine my life without them. I'm thankful every day and would not trade this life for a different one." Anita had embraced the life she had. Her apartment was the size of most kitchens; she was working full time; one child was on an oxygen machine; and both children had significant physical, mental, and emotional challenges. She didn't go out for fun but treasured her friendships and saw her children as amazing gifts. She was exhausted but consistently kept a positive attitude. She chose to truly appreciate what she had, and she noticed God's presence in her life. This helped her adjust her attitude and focus in parenting and life.

Few of us have to confront the kinds of challenges Anita was facing, but we all have difficulties. Difficulties can distract us and cause us to focus on ourselves. Gratitude helps us refocus on a bigger picture that includes others and God's sovereignty in our lives.

3. Take Pictures

At funerals, graduations, and weddings, I am consistently moved by the moments that give a glimpse into the larger story of a family's life. You see, these moments are like pictures, snapshots of a point in time. These captured moments are part of a larger experience. And that experience is part of several other stories weaving together within a much larger picture. This larger picture is the masterpiece of how God is weaving all these events together for our good and for the glory of His Kingdom.

We get glimpses into some of the highlights of each person's life, but we don't often get to see pictures of the moments of adversity that can shape lives and relationships.

As I mentioned in a previous chapter, I have traveled with a group of dads for the last few years into the Ansel Adams Wilderness. Each of the dads on the trip brings a son or daughter who is twelve years old or older. There are difficult challenges each parent–child pair faces, such as climbing, rappeling from a high cliff, and jumping into a freezing lake. The dads write blessings for their children, and the children write letters of encouragement to their dads. There are powerful moments of connection, and many pictures, both digital and mental, are taken. The pictures capture moments of adversity that each parent–child pair conquered. These moments strengthened their courage and relationship.

What if we faced day-to-day challenges in our lives this way? What if we took pictures of the helpful courage-building, relationship-building, character-building moments we inevitably will have as parents and families?

I challenge you to stop and take pictures, whether digital or mental, of these moments in the life of your family. Notice how each picture captures a single moment. With gratitude, consider each moment and all that it reveals about your family. Perhaps your family is growing in thoughtfulness or in compassion or helpfulness. Notice how the story of your family is fuller and richer when you picture these moments together, like a photo album of your family's history and growth.

Gratitude, essentially, is a way of seeing the world from multiple angles. It helps a person move past loss, adversity, difficulty, or challenge. Gratitude helps a person see that life eventually has an end, that each day is a gift, and that each day counts. David wrote, "O Lord, make me know my end and what is the measure of my days; let me know how fleeting I am!" (Psalm 39:4). In Psalm 90:12 Moses wrote, "So teach us to number our days, that we may present to You a heart of wisdom" (NASB).

Kids can be especially good at this kind of gratitude. They are amazed more easily than adults because they have had fewer life experiences. One evening not long ago, my daughter and I were jumping on the trampoline in our backyard when Lexi looked up and said, "I just love that star! It's always the first one to come out. It's so beautiful! It's my very favorite of all the stars in the sky!" She helped me stop and notice.

Lexi's response to the star reminded me that grateful people enjoy life. And God has given us plenty of wonderful things to enjoy. We lose sight of these everyday marvels when circumstances take over or when we're too busy. But the beauty is always there, even when we're not paying attention. That's why Paul reminds us to keep pulling our minds back to the things that are true, honorable, just, pure, lovely, and commendable (Philippians 4:8). That's why he tells us to give thanks in all circumstances (1 Thessalonians 5:18). As we've already seen, gratitude is a kind of "mental muscle" that has to be kept in shape with daily exercise.

Gratitude that gets exercised on a regular basis becomes an effective antidote to anxiety and fear. It enables you to see the whole universe from an entirely new perspective. It converts you from the pessimist who sees the glass as half-empty to the optimist who sees the glass as half-full. It makes it possible to see the potential in others instead of focusing on their flaws. It even inspires you to give thanks for those flaws since, without them, you'd have fewer opportunities to demonstrate grace, forgiveness, and love. Gratitude helps you embrace your own imperfections so that, in turn, you can embrace the imperfections of others.

You can transform your family relationships by asking yourself some simple questions: What am I focusing on when I look at my family? Do I only notice what they're not doing? Or do I focus on the good things they are doing? Is my first inclination to correct their flaws? Or am I instead quick to see the bigger picture of God's design and work in them and respond in gratitude?

Having an ongoing conversation with God about our families can help us to pull back and shift our perspectives away from nitpicky frustrations in order to see our family members through the lenses of love, joy, peace, patience, kindness, faithfulness, goodness, gentleness, and self-control, even in the midst of chaos and difficulty. That would certainly be cause for pictures!

4. Be Genuine

Genuine gratitude is expressed in genuine smiles (our brains positively respond to genuine smiles and ignore fake smiles), authentic hugs, and compliments that are true and based on fact, not just sweet-sounding words. Genuine gratitude comes across most effectively when you are able to accept and embrace the other person as a complete package, blemishes and all. In my experience as a counselor, I've seen case after case where genuine gratitude creates connection and trust between people.

The apostle Paul occupies a special place in the pages of Scripture as someone who expressed genuine gratitude in all kinds of circumstances, and we can learn much from his example. Even in the midst of trials, corrections, sufferings, and misfortunes, he had confidence that God was strengthening him. As a result, he was truly thankful in everything that came his way.

Paul wrote, "For the sake of Christ, then, I am content

with weaknesses, insults, hardships, persecutions, and calamities. For when I am weak, then I am strong" (2 Corinthians 12:10). It was this same attitude of gratitude that helped him write, "And we know that for those who love God all things work together for good, for those who are called according to his purpose" (Romans 8:28). Established firmly upon the solid rock of that conviction, Paul found it natural to exhort other Christians to be thankful (Colossians 3:15).

As a dad, I like to pause every once in a while and remind myself to be grateful for my children on this deep and authentic level. Sometimes when they're sleeping I'll slip into their bedrooms and pray by their bedsides, expressing my gratitude to God for His gift to me. It's like drinking water when I'm really thirsty. It refreshes my soul and resets my relationship with Alex and Lexi as almost nothing else can do. I believe this is because God has wired our brains to respond to gratitude as the body responds to

ACTIVITY

Chalk Pens

Use a chalk pen (or a dry-erase marker) to write notes to your kids on the bathroom or bedroom mirror. When I do this for my children, I write things I am thankful for or truths about who God has created each of them to be. I intentionally make each message unique to help each child see that my words are genuine.

Consider the messages we tell ourselves when we stand in front of the mirror. The mirror is where falsehoods are absorbed. It's where the negative things we think about ourselves take root in our minds. That's why this is the perfect place to tell the truth about who God has created your child to be and what He is doing through him or her.

rest, nourishment, and healing medicine. When we give genuine thanks, our brains are refreshed, reshaped, and redirected. Interestingly, research on gratitude throughout the past decade has reinforced this reality. God truly heals and strengthens a grateful mind, no matter how chaotic, tired, or broken it may be. God's Word tells us in Romans 12:9 to "let love be genuine." Paul provided a wonderful example of genuine love and thanksgiving. In the letters he wrote to various churches, he would tell them of his gratitude for their steadfastness, faithfulness, and endurance. He was genuine and passionate in his expression of gratitude toward God's people.

A study published in 2016 in the journal *NeuroImage* demonstrated conclusively that people who make a regular practice of expressing gratitude—especially those who formalize the process by recording things for which they're thankful in a written diary or journal—activated those parts of the brain associated with feeling and expressing empathy for others.[5] In other words, people who feel grateful are more likely to reach out to help others than those who don't. In the context of the family, that can translate into a greater degree of cooperation and a willingness to work together in the home. Parents can set the tone by being grateful and empathetic themselves, starting with their marriage. Consider what might happen if you and your spouse wrote notes of gratitude to one another that your children could observe. There's no better way for kids to learn positive behaviors and attitudes than by watching and mirroring Mom and Dad!

5. Be Patient

Patience fosters gratitude. It allows time to let emotions flow in order for you to more effectively manage your perceptions and your memories.

Research has shown that our brains are naturally more prone to remember bad things than good things. The brain is designed to, in milliseconds, draw from the past and anticipate the future while living in the present. It is designed to make quick judgments.

When the psalmist Asaph was tempted to give in to despair, he fought back by being patiently selective in his observations. He consciously pointed his mind toward God's larger story instead of getting caught up in his present circumstances. He wrote, " 'I will appeal to this, to the years of the right hand of the Most High.' I will remember the deeds of the LORD; yes, I will remember your wonders of old. I will ponder all your work,

The Peace Table

The peace table provides family members with an opportunity to share what they are thankful for and what they are frustrated with. It's all about making the home a better place and encouraging the growth of genuine gratitude in the heart of each person who lives there.

The first step is for each person to write down what he or she is thankful for. Second, each person can write down frustrations and suggest solutions.

Put some kind of container for the slips of paper in a prominent location in the house—maybe on the kitchen counter or table. Then set up a time once a week when you can all get together to discuss what's written, perhaps at dinner or over dessert.

First read the notes that

share thanksgiving and affirm your own genuine thanksgiving for these things.

Next, read the notes that share frustrations. Acknowledge feelings and affirm the intention of the family to work together to find solutions. Work together to agree on a solution and commit to follow through. Decide who's going to take action to make the plan work. Make a list of these tasks and the names of the people responsible for each one. Post it on your refrigerator.

When the goal is reached, do something to celebrate (get ice cream, play a game together, go to a movie, go out for dinner). The purpose is to create a family team effort toward gratitude, resolutions, and celebrations.

and meditate on your mighty deeds" (Psalm 77:10-12).

This psalm reminds me that some of the principles of positive psychology have been around for a long, long time! Asaph knew that the way to get his mind unstuck and get it out of feeling overwhelmed and depressed was to remember times he had seen God at work.

The apostle Paul writes of a similar truth in Romans 12:2: "Be transformed by the renewal of your mind." This is not a quick process; it takes patience.

I vividly remember meeting with a teen boy who had just been released from the hospital. He had tried to take his own life but, thankfully, was unsuccessful. He came to my counseling office and said, "What a difference two weeks can make in life. I'm so glad I didn't kill myself." He said life had drastically changed in two weeks. He had come to realize that the circumstances of life, whether good or bad, are not permanent. As he began to develop patience with others, life, and himself, he felt more grateful for life. He also learned to be patient with God's timing as God unfolds a grander story.

Memory is a highly technical video-playback system. You can choose which videos you want to see. There are mental, emotional, and physical benefits of remembering positive things. Be selective, and be careful about your interpretation.

Guide your mind toward recording, archiving, and celebrating your family's history. Be patient in what God is doing in your children and in your own life. The picture is unfolding.

A LIFE OF GRATITUDE

Those ancient Chinese and Egyptians were on to something profound when they started writing and sharing their papyrus thank-you notes. They knew, as people in every time and place have always known, that we never really experience life in its fullness until we've seen it clearly

New Year's Day Box
On New Year's Eve, many people reflect on the past year as they prepare to welcome the new year. Throughout the year you can use a box to collect items that reflect the memorable events of that year. You could collect pictures or small mementos from birthdays, vacations, sporting events, ballet recitals, dinners out, visits from relatives, Valentine's Day, Easter, Christmas—you name it. Stow all this stuff in your box as the days pass.

When New Year's Eve comes around, pull out the box and spend some time talking with your family about the events each item represents. There will be a lot to be thankful for. Reflect on what your family has conquered, persevered through, accomplished, and enjoyed along the way.

enough to give thanks for all it encompasses. That includes the bad as well as the good.

President John F. Kennedy put it this way: "As we express our gratitude, we must never forget that the highest appreciation is not to utter words, but to live by them."[6]

GRATITUDE

GRATITUDE is a choice—a decision to view the world & experiences through a lens of thankfulness.

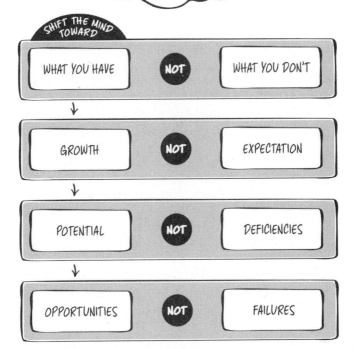

SHIFT THE MIND TOWARD

| WHAT YOU HAVE | NOT | WHAT YOU DON'T |

| GROWTH | NOT | EXPECTATION |

| POTENTIAL | NOT | DEFICIENCIES |

| OPPORTUNITIES | NOT | FAILURES |

BIG IDEA

- We never really experience life in its fullness until we've seen it clearly enough to give thanks for all it encompasses. That goes double for family life.
- Gratitude leads to contentment, health, humility, connection, peace & less stress.
- Gratitude takes practice and is an essential discipline.

ACTIONS

- Be a noticer
- Take pictures
- Be patient
- Be genuine
- Appreciate what you have

APPENDIX

Parental Concerns at Each Age and Stage

THROUGHOUT MY YEARS working with families and engaging with the latest research, I have found that all parents face unique challenges. My hope is that the seven traits of effective parenting will provide you with a template to work with at each age and stage of your child's development and the challenges you will face.

Below I have listed some of the more common concerns that research and my experience identify as challenges at each age and stage of your child's development.

EXPECTANT PARENTS

Expectant parents tend to be concerned about:

- the unknowns
- health—their own, as well as their child's
- work
- finances
- what to anticipate developmentally

If you are an expectant parent, you can apply the seven traits of effective parenting by the following:

- Be intentional about communication with each other as you prepare to have a baby.
- Work on being respectful to each other in your communication as you prepare for sleep deprivation and sharing chores.
- Think about the contributors versus consumers, encouragers versus discouragers, and influencers versus distractors in your own lives to see if steadfast love, respect, adaptability, intentionality, grace and forgiveness, boundaries and limits, and gratitude were modeled along the way.
- Discuss the parenting style you are most familiar with and explore what parenting style you want to strive to have in your home.
- Make an effort to grow in all seven traits as a team, just as athletes at training camp prepare for the regular season.

CHILDREN AGES 0-3

Parents of children ages 0–3 tend to be concerned about:

- their child's spiritual development and foundation
- their own sleep deprivation and their baby's sleep issues
- their child's defiant and out-of-control behaviors

- discipline—whether to spank or use time-outs
- their parenting styles and parenting differences
- the division of chores between parents
- busy schedules and routines
- their child's health
- whether to have a babysitter for their child

If you are parents of a 0- to 3-year-old child, you can implement the seven traits of effective parenting by the following:

- Show steadfast love by learning each other's parenting-style differences and respectfully looking for ways to work together as a team.
- Demonstrate respect in the way you communicate with your spouse and by carefully listening to and observing what your child is trying to communicate through crying and other behaviors.
- Set boundaries by establishing consistent corrections to certain behaviors and emotions.
- Offer grace by realizing that your spouse is not perfect and by encouraging rather than criticizing. Also, recognize that your child's crying and behavior issues may be due to hunger, discomfort, or a lack of sleep. You can see behavior issues as an opportunity for molding, building, and teaching in your child's life.
- Show gratitude by adopting the perspective that being a parent is a sacred blessing. Gratitude infuses patience into frustrating moments. Gratitude is also

the foundation to becoming a loving, respectful, and intentional parent and provides the fuel to get through sleep-deprived nights.

- Intentionally carve out time with your spouse and establish the schedules and routines that are needed for your home. Intentionality at this age and stage is also about developing habits and patterns for a spiritual foundation in your home, such as prayer, reading the Bible, going to church, and talking about God in everyday moments.

- Choose to be adaptable by maintaining an open and flexible mind toward the imperfections of being a parent to an infant or toddler. There will be a lot of messes, unexpected illnesses, and frustrating moments.

CHILDREN AGES 4-7

Parents of children ages 4–7 tend to be concerned about:

- spiritual development
- behavior issues
- discipline and boundaries
- cooperative play
- messiness
- their child's adjustment to school
- the division of chores in the house

- communication as a couple and sexual relationship as a couple
- differences in discipline

Children who are 4 to 7 years old:

- are active and love to move while learning, especially boys
- want to be helpers
- need direction, consistency, routines, clear rules, discipline, and predictability
- tend to challenge authority, but want to please and not disappoint
- want to do difficult things and try things for themselves
- are sensitive to criticism and want to do well
- tend to become bossy
- love playing in groups and are focused on friends
- can develop a strong sense of right and wrong
- are sometimes dramatic
- will sometimes say that things are unfair or complain about the rules
- can become moody and "stuck" emotionally

If you are parents of a 4- to 7-year-old child, you can apply the seven traits of effective parenting by the following:

- Give your child clear and consistent boundaries and limits.

- Let your child experience adversity, disappointment, failure, and challenge.
- Model respect toward others.
- Intentionally develop boundaries, limits, and balance for your home.
- Intentionally notice and discuss God's presence in your day-to-day lives.
- Intentionally pray and discuss God's Word together.
- Adapt to your child's personality and unique circumstances.
- Show steadfast love when your child disobeys or misbehaves at inconvenient times.
- Practice gratitude to help maintain perspective when things feel chaotic.
- Use grace and forgiveness to repair relationships in your home when things don't go right.

As you implement the seven traits of effective parenting, you can:

- provide structure
- provide opportunities to help, fail, and try new things
- help your child find age-appropriate challenges
- provide encouraging words
- help your child find God's presence in his or her life
- pray with your child and practice learning to listen to God

- be consistent with rules to help your child understand the purpose of boundaries and limits
- help your child learn to control his or her emotions, thoughts, needs, and wants
- laugh and play with your child, and bring goofiness and play into tasks that take a while to complete
- provide distractions when your child's brain (emotions) gets stuck

CHILDREN AGES 8-12

Parents of children ages 8–12 years old tend to be concerned about:

- their child's spiritual development
- "the Talk," sexuality, and guiding their child through puberty
- discipline and consistency
- parenting differences
- technology, entertainment, screen time, balance, and limits
- their child's friendships
- their relationship with their child (conflict, communication, time together)
- their child's sudden negativity toward self and others (especially self)
- emotional issues and inconsistencies
- whether it's good to have sleepovers

Children who are 8 to 12 years old tend to:

- love socializing and having friendships
- become quickly negative toward themselves
- complain
- have stronger sibling conflicts
- want others' approval and acceptance
- enjoy humor and playing jokes
- become more focused
- be less patient
- be more sensitive to criticism
- find ways around boundaries and limits
- observe and follow how their peers are pursuing spirituality

Parents of 8 to 12 year olds who want to address sex education, "the Talk," and guiding their children through puberty will apply the seven traits of effective parenting by the following:

- Model marital love and appropriate loving touch in the home.
- Discuss what steadfast love from God's perspective is all about.
- Teach about being a contributor to (noticer, builder, and connector) rather than a consumer of people. Find out more by taking the quiz at focusonthefamily.com/noticer-builder-connector-quiz/.

- Intentionally carve out time to pray and read God's Word together as a family.
- Point out God's creation, presence, and design.
- Intentionally discuss sexuality through the lens of Philippians 4:8.
- Model respect through your own sexuality (what you look at, what you listen to, how you touch your spouse, where you spend your time, how you talk about sex).
- Intentionally discuss and model gratitude for the gifts of sex and beauty in the way they were intended to be enjoyed through God's design.
- Apply grace as you recognize that managing puberty and sexuality is difficult.
- Be adaptable to questions coming at random times and to personality differences as sexuality is discussed.
- Be intentional in establishing and discussing boundaries and limits regarding media, dating, phones, and friendships.

As you implement the seven traits at this age and stage, you can:

- point out specifically what your child is doing well
- mentor your child in managing his or her attention and time
- help your child learn ways to own his or her faith, love others, serve others, and become aware of others' emotions

- teach your child to be a builder of himself or herself and others from a biblical perspective
- teach your child how to truly connect with others and how to help others connect
- make intentional relational time, involving dates, walks, playing games, tea, coffee, mealtimes, movies, and anything else you can think of
- teach your child how to handle failure, mistakes, losing, and adversity
- help your child notice and tap into his or her support system of coaches, teachers, friends, pastors, mentors, and parents
- reassure your child about his or her uniqueness
- point out to your child that being heroic means becoming the best version of who God created him or her to be
- teach your child about friendships and relationships
- be clear, consistent, and attentive in setting boundaries and limits
- enforce and follow through instead of arguing when the boundaries and limits are not followed

CHILDREN AGES 13-18

Parents of children ages 13–18 years old tend to be concerned about:

- their child's spiritual development and ownership
- communication, conflict resolution, and disagreements

- their child's relationships
- dating, sex, and moral standards
- technology, entertainment, and screen time
- pornography
- friendships, decision making, and peer influences
- preparation for college and adulthood
- mental health issues—depression, anxiety, and ADHD
- their child's life balance (work, sports, extracurricular activities, school, friends, dating, home, and responsibilities)

Children who are 13 to 18 years old tend to:

- take risks
- search for belonging
- love spending time with friends
- become involved in activities
- want time, attention, and approval from peers and friends
- be self-conscious and self-critical
- be critical and judgmental
- think they are adults and know everything
- become more easily and deeply overwhelmed and stressed
- challenge boundaries and limits
- want freedom and independence
- be insecure
- love novelty

- initially have a regression in maturity (sometimes becoming more immature than when they were at age 9 or 10) and then quickly mature into the responsibilities they own as they go further into adolescence
- enjoy goofiness and laughter
- want to be unique, yet part of trends
- be more easily influenced by culture, messages, trends, peers, coaches, and others outside of the home
- become more specialized in their interests

If you are parents of a teenager, you can apply the seven traits of effective parenting by the following:

- Model steadfast love toward one another.
- Show respect while you guide your teen through communication, conflict, relationships, dating, technology, phones, and entertainment.
- Be intentional about carving out time for spiritual development and conversations.
- Establish consistent and well-defined boundaries and limits that lead your child toward becoming an interdependent adult.
- Show and communicate gratitude for adversity, failure, and growth opportunities.
- Use grace and forgiveness to repair relationships and reconnect.
- Be adaptable to ever-shifting and crowded schedules, personality differences, and unexpected adversity.

As you implement the seven traits, you can:

- carve out intentional and consistent time with your teen (coffee, lunch, dinner, breakfast, walks, working out, hikes)
- listen attentively and remember what he or she said so that you can circle back and ask follow-up questions later
- model grace
- model love by how you love others, including your spouse
- model a trusting and active relationship with God
- lead consistent times of prayer and be aware of different ways God may have answered prayers
- help your child reflect on his or her own decision making, friendships, options, pursuits, and opinions
- help your child develop a deeper level of self-understanding
- help your child learn to define himself or herself as a follower of Christ and child of God, and not by what he or she does
- provide consistent boundaries and limits and discuss your child's purpose and path toward interdependence and true freedoms
- explore deeper topics and questions, such as, *What is beauty? What is freedom? How do we decide who is or isn't popular? What are the characteristics of a good friend? What does prayer do for the mind?*

- specifically and genuinely compliment your child according to who he or she is (character traits) and what he or she does (skills and talents)
- provide honest feedback with respect, grace, and love

ACKNOWLEDGMENTS

Thank you to Jim Ware, Randy Southern, and Beth Robinson as you helped me in shaping this book and getting it through the editing process. Editors who love God are like having God's angels working with you throughout the writing process. It is not an easy endeavor, but you helped me along the way.

Thank you to Willy Wooten who hired me in 2004 to work for the Focus on the Family counseling team and provided mentoring for me along the way. Willy Wooten and the counseling team at Focus on the Family were an incredible group to work with as we served in God's Kingdom.

Thank you to Jim Daly, the C-team, and the board at Focus on the Family for trusting that God has called me to serve as Vice President of Parenting and Youth in His ministry. What an honor it is to serve alongside each and every one of you and the entire staff. I am thankful to serve in an organization surrounded by such talented brothers and sisters in Christ who are dedicated to God's calling on their lives.

Thank you to the rolling credits in my life—the investors, encouragers, and influencers. It would take pages and pages to acknowledge all of you who have significantly contributed in some way or another to my story, from mentors, coaches, siblings, and teachers to bosses, coworkers, and neighbors. THANK YOU!

NOTES

CHAPTER 1: CONTRIBUTORS, ENCOURAGERS, AND INFLUENCERS

1. Monica Anderson and Jingjing Jiang, "Teens' Social Media Habits and Experiences," Pew Research Center Internet & Technology, November 28, 2018, http://www.pewinternet.org/2018/11/28/teens-social-media -habits-and-experiences/.
2. Globe Newswire, "45% of Teens Say They're Stressed 'All the Time,' Turn to Online Resources and Apps for Help Says Poll on Stress and Mental Health," February 21, 2018, https://globenewswire.com/news-release/2018 /02/21/1372739/0/en/45-of-Teens-Say-They-re-Stressed-All-the-Time-Turn -to-Online-Resources-and-Apps-for-Help-Says-Poll-on-Stress-and-Mental -Health.html.
3. Royal Society for Public Health, "#StatusofMind: Social Media and Young People's Mental Health and Wellbeing," 2018, https://www.rsph.org.uk/our -work/campaigns/status-of-mind.html.
4. Kristen Harrison, Lia Vallina, Amelia Couture, Halie Wenhold, and Jessica D. Moorman, "Sensory Curation: Theorizing Media Use for Sensory Regulation and Implications for Family Media Conflict," *Media Psychology* 22, no. 4 (2019): 653–88, doi: 10.1080/15213269.2018.1496024.
5. Kit K. Elam, Laurie Chassin, Nancy Eisenberg, and Tracy L. Spinrad, "Marital Stress and Children's Externalizing Behavior as Predictors of Mothers' and Fathers' Parenting," *Development and Psychopathology* 29, no. 4 (2017): 1305–1318, doi: 10.1017/S0954579416001322.

CHAPTER 2: ADAPTABILITY

1. "Adaptable Decision Making in the Brain," *ScienceDaily*, June 19, 2012, www.sciencedaily.com/releases/2012/06/120619225234.htm.
2. Matthew P. Walker, Conor Liston, J. Allan Hobson, and Robert Stickgold, "Cognitive Flexibility across the Sleep-Wake Cycle: REM-Sleep Enhancement of Anagram Problem Solving," *Cognitive Brain Research* 14, no. 3 (November 2002): 317–24, doi: 10.1016/S0926-6410(02)00134-9.

CHAPTER 3: RESPECT

1. Daniel A. Hughes and Jonathan Baylin, *Brain-Based Parenting: The Neuroscience of Caregiving for Healthy Attachment* (New York: W. W. Norton, 2012).
2. MIT News, "MIT Research—Brain Processing of Visual Information," December 19, 1996, http://news.mit.edu/1996/visualprocessing.
3. Susan Hagen, "The Mind's Eye," University of Rochester, 2012, http://www.rochester.edu/pr/Review/V74N4/0402_brainscience.html.
4. Roy Baumeister, Kathleen Vohs, and Dianne Tice, "The Strength Model of Self-Control," *Current Directions in Psychological Science* 16, no. 6 (December, 2007): 351–55, doi: 10.1111/j.1467-8721.2007.00534.x.
5. Sara Villanueva Dixon, Julia Graber, and Jeanne Brooks-Gunn, "The Roles of Respect for Parental Authority and Parenting Practices in Parent-Child Conflict among African American, Latino, and European American Families," *Journal of Family Psychology* 22, no. 1 (February, 2008): 1–10, doi: 10.1037/0893-3200.22.1.1.
6. Jack Zenger and Joseph Folkman, "The Ideal Praise-to-Criticism Ratio," *Harvard Business Review*, March 15, 2013, https://hbr.org/2013/03/the-ideal-praise-to-criticism.
7. Daniel. J. Siegel, *Pocket Guide to Interpersonal Neurobiology: An Integrative Handbook of the Mind* (New York: W. W. Norton, 2012).

CHAPTER 4: INTENTIONALITY

1. Carol Watson-Phillips, "Relational Fathering: Sons Liberate Dads," *The Journal of Men's Studies* 24, no. 3 (October 2016): 277–93, doi: 10.1177/1060826516661188.
2. Ibid.
3. Sharon Lawrence and Mary Plisco, "Family Mealtimes and Family Functioning," *The American Journal of Family Therapy* 45, no. 4 (June 2017): 195–205, doi: 10.1080/01926187.2017.1328991.
4. Reinhold Niebuhr, "Prayer for Serenity," retrieved from: https://www.celebraterecovery.com/resources/cr-tools/serenityprayer.

CHAPTER 5: STEADFAST LOVE

1. This section adapted from *Module 207: Bernard of Clairvaux on Love*, Christian History Institute, https://christianhistoryinstitute.org/study/module/bernard and Hal Runkel, *Screamfree Parenting: How to Raise Amazing Adults by Learning to Pause More and React Less* (New York: Harmony Books, 2008).
2. Jude Cassidy, Jason D. Jones, and Philip R. Shaver, "Contributions of Attachment Theory and Research: A Framework for Future Research,

Translation, and Policy," *Development and Psychopathology* 25, no. 4 (part 2) (November 2013): 1415–34, doi: 10.1017/S0954579413000692.

3. Judith Kay Nelson, "Laugh and the World Laughs with You: An Attachment Perspective on the Meaning of Laughter in Psychotherapy," *Clinical Social Work Journal* 36 (2008): 41–49, doi: 10.1007/s10615-007-0133-1.

CHAPTER 6: BOUNDARIES

1. Diana Baumrind, "Current Patterns of Parental Authority," *Developmental Psychology* 4, no. 1 (part 2) (1971): 1–103, doi: 10.1037/h0030372.

2. Johnmarshall Reeve, *Understanding Motivation and Emotion*, 6th ed. (Danvers, MA: John Wiley & Sons, 2014).

3. Avidan Milevsky, Melissa Schlechter, Sarah Netter, and Danielle Keehn, "Maternal and Paternal Parenting Styles in Adolescents: Associations with Self-Esteem, Depression and Life-Satisfaction," *Journal of Child and Family Studies* 16 (February 2007): 39–47, doi: 10.1007/s10826-006-9066-5.

4. Tori Rodriguez, "Harsh Parents Raise Bullies—So Do Permissive Ones," *Scientific American Mind*, September 1, 2016, https://www.scientific american.com/article/harsh-parents-raise-bullies-so-do-permissive-ones/.

5. Joy Gabrielli, Lisa Marsch, and Suzanne Tanski, "TECH Parenting to Promote Effective Media Management," *Pediatrics* 142, no. 1 (July 2018): e20173718, doi: 10.1542/peds.2017-3718.

CHAPTER 7: GRACE AND FORGIVENESS

1. Kirsten Weir, "Forgiveness Can Improve Mental and Physical Health: Research Shows How to Get There," *Monitor on Psychology* 48, no. 1 (January 2017): 30–33, https://www.apa.org/monitor/2017/01/ce-corner.

2. Gary Smalley and John Trent, *The Two Sides of Love: The Secret to Valuing Differences* (Colorado Springs, CO: Focus on the Family, 2019).

3. Lisa Belkin, "The Only Parenting 'Philosophy' You Really Need," *Huffington Post*, October 4, 2013, https://www.huffpost.com/entry/the-only-parenting -philosophy-you-really-need_n_4040706.

4. J. P. Moreland and Klaus Issler, *The Lost Virtue of Happiness: Discovering the Disciplines of the Good Life* (Colorado Springs, CO: NavPress, 2006).

5. Lesley Brose, Mark Rye, Catherine Lutz-Zois, and Scott Ross, "Forgiveness and Personality Traits," *Personality and Individual Differences* 39, no. 1 (July 2005): 35–46, doi: 10.1016/j.paid.2004.11.001.

6. Loren Toussaint, Shanmukh Kamble, Justin C. Marschall, and Deepti B. Duggi, "The Effects of Brief Prayer on the Experience of Forgiveness: An American and Indian Comparison," *International Journal of Psychology* 51, no. 4 (August 2016): 288–95, doi: 10.1002/ijop.12139.

CHAPTER 8: GRATITUDE

1. Robert Emmons, *Thanks!: How the New Science of Gratitude Can Make You Happier* (New York: Houghton Mifflin, 2007).
2. Mackenzie Dawson, "Parenting in a Fakebook World: How Social Media Is Affecting Your Parenting," *Parents*, June 28, 2015, https://www.parents.com/parenting/better-parenting/style/how-social-media-is-affecting-your-parenting.
3. "A Mother's Life-Preserver," The National WWII Museum, May 12, 2012, http://nww2m.com/2012/05/a-mothers-life-preserver/.
4. J. P. Moreland and Klaus Issler, *The Lost Virtue of Happiness: Discovering the Disciplines of the Good Life* (Colorado Springs, CO: NavPress, 2006).
5. Prathik Kini, Joel Wong, Sydney McInnis, Nicole Gabana, and Joshua Brown, "The Effects of Gratitude Expression on Neural Activity," *NeuroImage* 128, (2016): 1–10, doi: 10.1016/j.neuroimage.2015.12.040.
6. John F. Kennedy, Thanksgiving Day Proclamation, November 4, 1963, BrainyQuote.com, https://www.brainyquote.com/quotes/quotes/j/johnfkenn105511.html.